REDEMPTİVE SUFFERİNG

*Lessons Learned from
the Garden of Gethsemane*

LESLİE MONTGOMERY

CROSSWAY BOOKS

A PUBLISHING MINISTRY OF
GOOD NEWS PUBLISHERS
WHEATON, ILLINOIS

Redemptive Suffering

Copyright © 2006 by Leslie Montgomery

Published by Crossway Books
  A publishing ministry of Good News Publishers
  1300 Crescent Street
  Wheaton, Illinois 60187

All rights reserved. No part of this publication may be reproduced, stored in a retrieval system or transmitted in any form by any means, electronic, mechanical, photocopy, recording or otherwise, without the prior permission of the publisher, except as provided by USA copyright law.

Cover design: Josh Dennis

Cover illustration: Jessica Dennis

Cover photos: iStock

First printing, 2006

Printed in the United States of America

Unless otherwise indicated, Scripture quotations are taken from *The Holy Bible: English Standard Version*®. Copyright © 2001 by Crossway Bibles, a publishing ministry of Good News Publishers. Used by permission. All rights reserved.

Scripture quotations indicated as from the NIV are taken from *The Holy Bible: New International Version*®. Copyright © 1973, 1978, 1984 by International Bible Society. Used by permission of Zondervan Publishing House. All rights reserved. The "NIV" and "New International Version" trademarks are registered in the United States Patent and Trademark Office by International Bible Society. Use of either trademark requires the permission of International Bible Society.

Scripture quotations indicated as from the NKJV are taken from *The Holy Bible: The New King James Version,* copyright © 1982 by Thomas Nelson, Inc. Used by permission.

Library of Congress Cataloging-in-Publication Data
Montgomery-Anderson, Leslie, 1967–
    Redemptive suffering : lessons learned from the Garden of Gethsemane / Leslie Montgomery.
      p. cm.
    ISBN 13: 978-1-58134-794-4 (tpb)
    ISBN 10: 1-58134-794-4 (tpb)
      1. Jesus Christ—Prayer in Gethsemane. 2. Gethsemane, Garden of.
    3. Jesus Christ—Passion. I. Title
    BT435.M65   2006
    232.96—dc22   2006011338

ML		16	15	14	13	12	11	10	09	08	07	06
15	14	13	12	11	10	9	8	7	6	5	4	3	2	1

To and for those who have lost hope in the midst of suffering.
From someone who's been there and back.

"Many are the afflictions of the righteous, but
the Lord delivers him out of them all."

P SALM 34:19

Contents

THANK-YOUS

It is impossible to thank *everyone* who has been instrumental in my growth and healing over the years, but there are some I absolutely cannot avoid mentioning. Two of these are Tom and Betty Tyndall. They gave me spiritual CPR through prayer and support during some of the darkest moments of my life. I am eternally grateful that the Lord has brought them into my life as spiritual parents.

I'd like to thank the pastoral "team" that has unknowingly passed the baton on to others during different times of my spiritual journey. Each one of you taught me invaluable lessons from the pulpit and through your own walk, leaving me hungering and thirsting for more of Jesus and for more healing. Don Finto and Stephen Mansfield from Belmont Church in Nashville, Tennessee helped build a strong spiritual foundation. Chris Williamson from Strong Tower Bible Church in Franklin, Tennessee believed that even a baby Christian had something to offer the Body of Christ, and his love and passion for Jesus spread like a wildfire into my soul. Dr. Bill Swegart from Buena Vista, Colorado taught me that Jesus wasn't a doormat and didn't call me to be one either. The life and walk of Doug Hazelstein from Christian Life Fellowship in Ontario, Oregon demonstrate the love and grace of Jesus, and his sense of humor is downright belly-aching. And last but not least, Pastor Dallas Anderson of the Billy Graham Center, my life-partner, best friend, and covering. You're my hero (Ecclesiastes 4:9-12).

Other pastors and leaders who have been instrumental along my journey include my personal friends and colleagues Dr. Ed Murphy, a spiritual warfare pioneer, Dr. Neil Anderson, a man who has shown millions freedom in Christ, and Norm Wright, whose love, acceptance, and mentoring have been invaluable to me.

Also, I'd like to thank my "spiritual fathers in the Lord" whom I'll meet on the other side of eternity—Charles Spurgeon, Smith Wigglesworth, C. S. Lewis, Andrew Murray, and E. M. Bounds. I have so many questions for the five of you!

Thanks also go to my dad, Art, who single-handedly proved to me before I became a believer that love in the present has the power to heal and conquer the hatred of the past.

My gratitude also goes to Terry MacAlmon, whose music fed my soul during the writing of this book. I'm also eternally grateful to the Third Day guys who, from the time of my conversion in 1993, have nourished my spirit and rocked my world with their music. Amazingly, you can say in three minutes what takes me an entire book!

I can't not include Molly Walker and Linda Collins who were my voice in one of the darkest moments in my life and held my hands up for battle when I didn't have the strength to do so myself. Thank you for going above and beyond the call of duty.

Jack and Kay Becker spiritually adopted me as their daughter in the Lord and are an excellent reflection of Jesus in all they say and do. I'm honored to be a part of their "family."

I also want to thank my Crossway "crew"—Allan Fisher, Jill Carter, and especially Randy Jahns, who from the onset of our collaborations have shared my vision and passion for Jesus and my desire to share the healing found in God's infallible Word, the Bible. I've never worked with such an incredible group of folks who have so much integrity and character (not to mention humor). I count you all among my greatest blessings. Special thanks to Ted Griffin, who does such excellent work editing my projects, taking special care to keep my sense of humor, passion, and personality in my work on behalf of our King.

Thanks to Joe-daddy and Juli Recla, with whom the Lord knitted my heart over the last year. "His banner over me is love" (Solomon's bride).

Thanks to John and Shirley Larson, who so generously opened their home up to me, welcoming me so graciously into their family. You encourage me with your willingness to love so freely. May God bless you a hundredfold.

Above all, I thank the Lord of my soul, Jesus, who continues to woo this brokenhearted child into his presence so that I might grow in spiritual stature and ultimately reflect his glory. There's nothing I enjoy more than dwelling in your presence.

Introduction

There is no greater agony than bearing an untold story inside of you.
MAYA ANGELOU

I hate suffering. As much as I have suffered in life, you'd think I'd have it down to a science by now. It's not that I've endured more or worse things than anyone else, mind you. It's just that it's been a constant companion in my thirty-nine years, like an ever-present shadow. Suffering and I have a love-hate relationship. Sometimes I've asked it to stay with me—for weeks, months, or years at a time—to bathe me in victimization and self-pity. Other times I've hated it with every fiber of my being, wishing it would disappear into the unknown and relieve me of its persevering voice that relentlessly controls and torments my emotions.

Unbelievers and Christian believers address suffering from opposite sides of the spectrum. The nonbeliever relies on a number of worldly options to help him or her cope. Alcohol, drugs, food, sex, money, and secular counseling are just a few things I've unsuccessfully tried in the past—choices that left me suffering even more without a sense of hope. As believers our hope is in the Lord, and thus we must forsake worldly options and cling to Jesus for relief from pain, grief, and sorrow. Sometimes he may use tools such as Christian counseling to help us as we grapple with our sorrows, but only after we've first and foremost submitted our pain to him.

When I became a believer thirteen years ago I heard my new brothers and sisters in the Lord say things like "Suffering as a Christian is inevitable" and "We should rejoice in our sufferings" and "Suffering is good because it produces endurance." I thought I'd been adopted into a family of sadomasochists! God made me a visual person, and I could not conceive how I would ever embrace suffering as if it were a long-lost friend in whom I found great joy. Nor could I grasp the concept that suffering would be worth the privilege of being able to put the word *endurance* on my list of personal character traits. I would have gladly exchanged all the endurance I'd ever gained in life just to be rid of the inevitable agony that accompanies it.

So the idea of finding joy in the midst of sorrow was totally contrary to every fiber of my body. Cognitively it seemed absurd, making no sense to my finite mind. I lived from this perspective as a believer for nine years, believing that God's view on suffering was one of those things I'd never grasp here on earth. It was, however, one of those topics at the top of my list of things to talk with him about on the other side of eternity. Then three specific incidents in my life directly and precisely challenged that lifetime perspective of pain and suffering.

The first event occurred when I was writing my first book in the, *Were It Not for Grace* series. That project included a great deal of research as well as interviews about how prominent women of God had overcome difficult circumstances in life through their faith in God. As I did research on Condoleezza Rice and the death of her parents, I was impressed. She appeared to be a godly woman who loved the Lord passionately. I felt a connection with her immediately especially since we had two very important things in common—a passion and love for Jesus Christ and shoes! Then Bobbi Brunzell, an employee and a member of Menlo Park Presbyterian Church in Menlo Park, California sent me three tapes of Condoleezza talking to that church's congregation. One of the tapes specifically talked about the struggle she went through after the loss of her parents, John and Angelina Rice.

In the middle of that first tape I heard Condoleezza say, "It is a privilege to struggle." I stopped the tape. *Did I just hear her say it's a privilege to struggle?* I thought to myself. I rewound the tape and listened to it again. *Yes!* I answered myself. *She said it is a privilege to struggle!* I was mortified! I shook my head back and forth in disagreement. *This woman is instrumental in running our country,* I thought, *and she's crazy!* As I listened and re-listened to her story, my heart softened. Although I didn't understand why, what she was saying made sense and began slowly descending into my heart. Looking back, I can see that was the beginning of a new chapter in my walk with God.

Shortly after writing Condoleezza's story, I was faced with what appeared to be an insurmountable situation in my own life. It involved my then eighteen-year-old son, Paul. Paul is mentally ill and has been tormented with schizophrenia for most of his life. As a mother, it has been devastating to me to watch this talented young man mentally deteriorate over the years. Over a ten-year period of time, he has gone from being a genius (literally—184 IQ) to having, in many ways, the mentality of an eight-year-old. To make matters worse, he is plagued every moment of every day by auditory and visual hallucinations. Can you imagine never having peace and quiet, never having the ability to distinguish between reality and delusions? As a mother, I have rarely felt so helpless. While medication has at times helped Paul's hallucinations diminish, they have never disappeared entirely. As a result, Paul vacillates between suicidal/homicidal inclinations and what appears to be a meditative trance and excessively writing what the voices are telling him in a screenplay format. Unfortunately, these voices mislead him to say and do inappropriate things that jeopardize his safety and the safety of others.

Shortly after his eighteenth birthday, Paul had a psychotic break and lost all concept of what little reality he was clinging to. One day he just woke up, dressed himself in a T-shirt, shorts, and flip-flops, and left our home in Colorado without saying a word to anyone. I was devastated, to say the least, aware of his fragile state of mind and fearing the worst. I turned my anger and agony on God. Not only did I bathe in fear and sorrow, I swam laps in it, assuring that I remained drenched in pain twenty-four hours a day. The problem wasn't the situation itself because as a believer I could rely on God to comfort me during this time—if I so chose. The problem was that I am a control freak, and I had no control of the pain and fear I was experiencing, nor did I have control of my son's whereabouts. Suddenly the rubber hit the road in my spiritual walk with God. I knew his Word inside and out, but would I use it in this dire state of mind?

Raised in a dysfunctional home where sex abuse and physical abuse were the norm, I learned to believe the lie that if I could control the circumstances around me, I could protect myself from all aspects of suffering. Although that wasn't really the case, I spent a great deal of energy trying to manipulate situations and those around me as a survival mechanism in order to minimize the pain I experienced in life. One way I did this was by avoiding intimacy at all costs with everyone, including God. Don't get me wrong—I loved the Lord and spent a great deal of time with him every day, but I always kept him and other important people in my life at arm's length, believing this would increase my odds of avoiding pain.

I called the police, put out a missing person's report on Paul, and put all of his friends and our family on alert in case they miraculously heard from him. I went online and put my son on every prayer list I could find. Then I had to wait in agonizing and relentless pain every day, one after the other. For hours and hours each day I would wonder, *Is Paul dead or alive? Will he be able to grasp enough reality to remember who he is? Where he's from? How to get home? That his mom loves him? Why has God allowed this to happen? What if someone abuses him?* I have never cried more in my life as I grieved the what-ifs and whys.

In order to retain my own sanity, I was forced to find some hope to hang on to. God has been so faithful in my life and has never forsaken me; so I instinctively turned to him and his Word. Never in all my life have I ever been so dependent on anything or anyone as I became on God at that time. I knew I'd go off the deep end of sorrow if I loosened my grip on the prayers and his promises that kept us connected. I knew that he was not promising me that my son would be returned to me or even that Paul would be cared for appropriately for that matter, but God did promise to spend every minute of every day with me as I grieved.

I spent hours upon hours talking to God every day, week after week. I slept very little during the months that followed, my grief and fear awaking me and refusing to allow me to rest. But I pressed on, combating the lies that the enemy whispered to me in the long, dark hours of the night, depending on God's promises to comfort me. It was the hardest thing I've ever gone through. Coming from someone who endured years of abuse as a child, chronic depression that led to multiple suicide attempts, and the loss of several loved ones, that is a significant statement. My children, Charlene and Paul, were my world, and when they suffered, I did too.

After Paul had been gone about five months, I fell on my face in weariness and sorrow. For all those months my prayer had been that the Lord would bring my son home so he could get the care he needed. But now, in complete exhaustion, I could not ask that anymore. Although I began to lose hope, I also knew that the Spirit of God was interceding for me in ways that I was not able to in my weak state. I didn't know what to pray for anymore, but he did (Romans 8:26).

In my fragile state I cried out to God and asked him if he would just let me know if Paul was dead or alive. It was okay if God didn't bring him back home. I knew Paul would be in his hands, but I pleaded for him to somehow reveal to me if Paul was alive. I fell asleep on the floor and slept sixteen hours straight, awaking to the peace that surpasses all understanding (Philippians 4:7). I wanted to put a meaning behind that peace. Did it mean that Paul was alive? Did it mean he was in heaven with God? God gave me no clarification at that time, so I was forced to just dwell in the comforting river of peace that was present.

Two weeks later I felt the Holy Spirit prompting me to e-mail Paul at his old Internet address from years before. *Yeah, right! This isn't God speaking,* I thought. *Paul's a homeless schizophrenic who doesn't have a computer! I'm NOT going to e-mail him,* I argued. It would be a ludicrous thing to do—e-mailing a homeless person. The idea made no sense whatsoever. But for the next two weeks the Holy Spirit kept prompting me to e-mail my son. Every time I refused. Have you ever had a wrestling match with God? Let me save you some time and let you in on a little secret: he always wins! Finally, at two o'clock one morning I awoke—wide-awake—prompted by the Holy Spirit to send Paul an e-mail at that very moment. In frustration I pulled back the covers, got out of bed, went to the computer, and reluctantly sent Paul an e-mail asking him to contact me if he received the message. I typed in my phone number and told him to call collect. After I sent the e-mail, I went back to bed.

When I woke up a couple of hours later, I was prompted to check my e-mail. I was ecstatic when I saw a returned e-mail from my son! It was a short note telling me he was on a "spiritual trek for God" and was fulfilling a mission as instructed by the voices. I immediately e-mailed him back and gave him my address and phone number again, instructing him to print my message and take it to the nearest police station. Within an hour I got a call from a New York City police officer who was sitting next to Paul!

I filled the police in on Paul's mental condition, and they said they'd keep him with them and feed him and take care of him until I could get him home. If you know New York City at all, this is a miracle in itself. Literally thousands of mentally ill homeless people wander the streets there. Because of that, the police are unable to make practical accommodations for them, especially during the winter months. At ten o'clock the next evening my son was returned home and was hospitalized so he could get the care he so desperately needed.

Now let me share the rest of this miraculous story. After Paul became somewhat stabilized in the hospital, I asked him how he checked his e-mail and what prompted him to do so. In a brief, sane moment (and I assure you that such moments are fleeting and rare during a psychotic break), he said he heard a *new* voice in his head, one he'd never heard before. It told him to walk to Times Square in downtown New York. When he got there, a man had a bench set up with computers on it. The "new voice" he was hearing told him to check his e-mail, and the man gave him permission to do so, thus leading him to contact me and return home to obtain medical care.

During the six months Paul had been gone, he had been in several different states. It was obvious to the police and any other person who came across Paul on the street begging for food that he was not in his right mind. One police department even kept him in jail overnight merely for observation, and he had been hospitalized in four mental hospitals along the way in different states. When he first arrived in New York City, he stayed in a homeless shelter for children. When the staff counselor asked if he had any family she could call, he answered, "My father was killed in a car accident, my mother was brutally murdered, and I have no siblings." None of this was true. They could tell Paul was men-

INTRODUCTION

tally ill, but they had no resource for contacting me. God was the only option.

Without a doubt, the "new voice" that Paul had heard prompting him to check his e-mail was the Holy Spirit miraculously answering my prayer. Looking back over the period of time that Paul was gone, I see that in my agony over my son, I was forced to cling to God in ways I never had before. The intimacy I developed with my Father in heaven during that time was something I honestly would never have pursued on my own. Knowing this, God allowed a situation to occur in my life that brought me so much pain and sorrow that I was forced to push through all my self-protective barriers into a level of intimacy with him merely to survive.

For the following fourteen months Paul was in and out of the mental hospital, eventually ending up in a treatment center for the mentally ill. On January 30, 2004 Paul had yet another psychotic break and walked away from treatment without notifying anyone. This time he was gone for five months. During this second absence I handled things very differently than during the first incident.

At first I thought that maybe Paul's return to me after his first psychotic break (as hard as it was to deal with) was the Lord's way of giving me one last opportunity to see my son. On the other hand, I believed that the Lord might intervene again and bring him back home in another miraculous way, which he did. The agony and grief that I experienced the second time was no less than it was after his first absence. The difference for me was that I was close enough to God to know that while I had no guarantee my son would return, I did have the promise that God wouldn't forsake me as I grappled with the pain—regardless of the outcome. The second time I had the peace of God that surpasses all understanding from day one, knowing and trusting that God would meet my needs as well as Paul's.

Instead of the what ifs and whys, I told myself, *You've been here before. God did not leave you or forsake you then. Instead you grew closer to him. You lived through it, and you will survive this too, as long as you cling to God.* I didn't know where my son was, what he was doing, whether or not he had food, whether he was cold or clothed, or whether or not he had a place to lay his head, but God did, and I *had* to trust him. God was faithful. I don't say that because he brought my son home a second time under equally miraculous circumstances, but because he never left me or forsook me, instead comforting me every moment of the journey. Part of the reason I experienced peace that surpassed understanding from the onset of Paul's second absence was because I *allowed* God to minister to me from the beginning rather than trying to deal with the pain, fear, and anguish on my own.

The story with Paul may not end at his return the second time. Young schizophrenics are notorious for running, and Paul may leave again someday. My faith in God cannot depend on whether or not my son leaves or returns again. Instead I must know that regardless of what the future holds, my Father in heaven will go through it with me, no matter how difficult the unknown may be.

The final instrumental circumstance that occurred was the encouragement from others to write a book on suffering. When *Were It Not for Grace* was written and the twelve women featured in it told of different difficult circumstances they have endured through their faith, I was encouraged to write about my own struggles throughout my life. To those who knew me best, the book of stories I wrote about other women and their tragedies and triumphs left out one very crucial thing—the heart, passion, and story that ran thick through my blood. They wanted me to share my story. The problem was, I was afraid to. I feared I wouldn't be able to articulate the theology of sorrow in a way that others would grasp and was fearful that my own sorrows paled in comparison to those of others, let alone the examples in the Bible.

As I prayed and sought wisdom from God, the Holy Spirit led me to Jesus' time in the Garden of Gethsemane, the place where Jesus chose to spend time in prayer the night before he was arrested. I had read the story a hundred times, knowing full well that Jesus suffered deeply there. But as I read it again, scales dropped from my eyes, and I saw the Garden of Gethsemane in a new light. Jesus' suffering there was unbearable from a human perspective, but that is just a glimmer of a much bigger picture. Our Savior chose Gethsemane for a reason, and in this book I will show you why. Not only did he experience sorrow there but a myriad of other emotions as well, and we will explore them and how they relate to our own pain. It was there in the Garden of Gethsemane that Jesus, the Son of Man, made some crucial decisions. We will examine those decisions and explore the same choices we have as we grapple with our pain and suffering. And finally we will see how Jesus Christ rejoiced in his suffering and will come to an understanding of why we are told and equipped to do the same.

So I have come to realize that Condoleezza Rice isn't crazy—she just knew the secret to suffering. It *is* a privilege to struggle, and as she said later, "Struggle and sorrow are not license to give way to self-doubt, self-pity, and defeat, but are an opportunity to find a renewed spirit and strength to carry on."

Within these pages I will share that secret with you, praying that you will find it as freeing and refreshing as those who have gone before you. Do not stop reading God's Word until you grasp this truth: "But rejoice insofar as you share Christ's sufferings, that you may also rejoice and be glad when his glory is revealed" (1 Peter 4:13). To rejoice in our suffering is not an unattainable goal or expectation that God has given to trap us in a web of inadequacy and incompetence but is instead a key that opens the door to freedom from a misery, agony, and anguish that cannot be comforted. So walk with me, dear friend. Let me lead the way down a path that is well worn by those who have gone before us and who have personally tasted joy in the midst of suffering.

Jesus himself must give you access to the wonders of Gethsemane: as for me, I can but invite you to enter the garden, bidding you put your shoes from off your feet, for the place whereon we stand is holy ground. I am neither Peter, nor James, nor John, but one who would fain like them drink of the Master's cup, and be baptized with his baptism.

CHARLES SPURGEON,
METROPOLITAN TABERNACLE PULPIT,
FEBRUARY 8, 1863

Jesus in Gethsemane— A Harmony of the Gospels

And Jesus went, as was his custom, to the Mount of Olives, and the disciples followed him. He went out with his disciples across the Kidron Valley, where there was a garden, which he and his disciples entered. And they went to a place called Gethsemane. And he said to his disciples, "Sit here, while I go over there and pray."

And taking with him Peter and the two sons of Zebedee, he began to be sorrowful and greatly distressed and troubled. Then he said to them, "My soul is very sorrowful, even to death; remain here, and watch with me."

And he withdrew from them about a stone's throw, and knelt down and prayed, saying, "My Father, if it be possible, let this cup pass from me; nevertheless, not as I will, but as you will." And there appeared to him an angel from heaven, strengthening him. And being in an agony he prayed more earnestly; and his sweat became like great drops of blood falling down to the ground. And he came to the disciples and found them sleeping, and he said to Peter, "Simon, are you asleep? Could you not watch one hour? Watch and pray that you may not enter into temptation. The spirit indeed is willing, but the flesh is weak."

Again, for the second time, he went away and prayed, "My Father, if this cannot pass unless I drink it, your will be done." And again he came and found them sleeping, for their eyes were very heavy, and they did not know what to answer him.

So, leaving them again, he went away and prayed for the third time, saying the same words again. And he came the third time and said to them, "Are you still sleeping and taking your rest? It is enough; the hour has come. The Son of Man is betrayed into the hands of sinners. Rise, let us be going; see, my betrayer is at hand." (Matthew 26:36-46; Mark 14:32-42; Luke 22:39-46; John 18:1)

THE PSYCHOLOGY OF SORROW

Quiet and sincere sympathy is often the most welcome and efficient consolation to the afflicted. Said a wise man to one in deep sorrow, "I did not come to comfort you; God only can do that; but I did come to say how deeply and tenderly I feel for you in your affliction."

TRYON EDWARDS (1809-1894)

We all have a Gethsemane—that is, a place and time in our lives when we face sorrow on the deepest level—a place of crisis, grief, anguish, excruciating pain, and loss. It's a time of separation, a tearing, or the ending of a relationship with someone or something that causes us to stop in our spiritual tracks and look more closely at who we are, our circumstances, and those around us. It brutally exposes what we honestly believe to be true in regard to God and his Word.

Our own private Gethsemane, like the garden where Jesus spent the night before his arrest, is often in some sense a calm before the storm, though also an intense trial in itself; but as excruciating as it is, we know there is more agony to come on an even greater scale. So when we are faced with a Gethsemane experience, it's not unusual to feel as though we are standing in the path of a tornado that is consuming everything in its way. After the torrential rains hit and the center of the storm finally touches down in our lives and clashes with what we perceive to be reality, everything and everyone in our lives becomes ineffective in their ability to comfort our pain as our whole world seems to be falling apart around us.

Divorce, sexual abuse, death, domestic violence, sickness, infertility, betrayal, financial loss, addiction, mental illness, war, and loss of employment are just a few out of thousands of circumstances that can cause such agonizing pain. When we consider catastrophic events like 9-11, the tsunami of 2004, and the Holocaust, we realize that grief and sorrow can affect millions of people at once and, like a rock thrown into a tranquil body of water, can cause ripples of pain that affect generations of people.

Against popular belief, pain, sorrow, and suffering occur in places as affluent as the White House, as lavish as a palace, as ordinary as a suburban household, or as cruel as the inner city. It doesn't matter if you're rich or poor, black or white, Hispanic or Asian. We all learn individually and as a family, as a nation and as a world, that suffering is inevitable, leading its victims to question God's goodness, power, and faithfulness.

- How could a God who loves me allow me to be sexually abused?
- He was such a righteous man—why did he have to die so young?
- God took my babies from me, knowing it would destroy me. Why?
- Where was God when that car accident took my husband and left me with four children to raise alone?
- Why did I survive the accident when everyone around me died?
- Why me, God? Why did you make me unable to bear children?
- How could God allow my mother to suffer for so long when she was so faithful to him all those years?

These are just a few of the questions I've heard from people I've counseled and prayed for over the years. They are valid questions, and those asking them should not be ashamed for expressing their pain and questioning their current circumstance in this way. It's unfortunate, however, that those who suffer are not always told that it's okay to share their pain. Out of pure ignorance, believers often give damaging answers when questions like these are expressed. I've heard people say insensitive things like, "God allowed you to be sexually abused to lead you to himself" or "It's okay that your husband died. At least he's in heaven now" or "Your children are in a better place" or "It's okay that you can't have children—you can always adopt" or "God won't give you more than you can handle" or "Haven't you ever read Job? He didn't complain, and he lost all ten of his kids." These responses leave the afflicted confused, guilty, and vulnerable to even more sorrow. Theologically, such answers may or may not be correct, but the starkness of simplistic clichés when someone is experiencing such trauma is insensitive, uncaring, and unappreciated to say the least.

There is no perfect response to someone else's pain because although we may be able to relate to it to some extent, we cannot really understand it. Because we have not experienced the other person's life, because we do not have their hormonal makeup, generational genes, or the tools they have gathered throughout life to sift through the ruins of various difficulties, because we have not shared the events in their lives that have made them who they are, because we are unable to fully understand their strengths and weaknesses, and because we cannot measure sorrow, we really have no right to dictate how they ought to feel about, experience, and overcome pain. To add shame and guilt to an already existing wound is comparable to throwing gas on a raging fire or rubbing salt in an open wound—it's unbearable and can keep the one experiencing it in a self-defeating spiritual spiral.

Consider two individuals of the same gender and age. Each loses a father to cancer. Both are traumatized by their grief. However, one is able to proceed through the stages of grief (denial, anger, bargaining, depression, acceptance) in a healthy way in an adequate amount of time. The other individual bathes in his (or her) grief, spending the rest of his days responding to life out of this wounded state, never really moving through the stages of grief, just dog-paddling between them at various times. We all know people like these two individuals. What's the difference?

The person who was able to process his (or her) grief may have had a stable home environment. Perhaps he was raised knowing his father loved him and had a saving relationship with Christ. He may have other family members who are equally healthy and are supportive to his needs and grief. He is able to talk about his pain to both God and others as he works through the loss of his father. The other person, however, may have not been raised in a healthy home. He (or she) may have watched his father profess to get saved at some point but also watched him backslide, and thus he is unsure of his father's spiritual health at the time of his death. Perhaps he has unresolved issues from his childhood, is hanging on to unforgiveness toward his father, and hasn't talked with him for years. Maybe his family is equally as angry and is unsupportive. As a result, he may unconsciously believe that he deserves to suffer and thus spends the rest of his life in a self-destructive, emotional tailspin.

Which one of these people's grief is worse? Neither. They have both experienced a devastating loss. However, one had the tools and support to work through his (or her) emotions, while the other did not. Research has shown the same scenario with Viet Nam vets. How could two men be in the same platoon, see and hear the same things, yet have such opposite responses to their circumstances? One is able to move beyond his experience and have a somewhat normal life, while the other spends the rest of his life in and out of mental hospitals, has recurring nightmares, suffers from post-traumatic stress disorder, is dependent on antidepressants and anti-anxiety medication, and perhaps even ends up committing suicide.

At some point in each of our lives, if not on numerous occasions, we will suffer sorrow. How we respond not only during the storms of life but also in the aftermath of our loss ultimately depends on the resources we have obtained through our relationship with Christ prior to that tragedy, as well as the tools he has equipped us to learn how to use in the midst of the trial. Equally so, we will also be the tools God uses to minister to others who are experiencing agonizing loss. Our success in compassionately supporting the sufferer will also ultimately depend on the resources we have obtained through our relationship with Christ. Thus, whether we are the sufferer or the comforter, Jesus must be our example.

Suffering is not something anyone looks forward to experiencing from the sidelines or as an actual participant. But because it's an inevitable part of life, we must learn to deal with it so we can grow through the experience and learn whatever God desires to teach us through it. As we mature in our relationship with Jesus Christ, we will come to understand the relationship between human suffering and God's power and love. In an effort to help attain this knowledge, we will look at the details of our Savior's example of suffering in some of the most horrific circumstances ever recorded. We will see how he was comforted during that time and the example he left for us as to where we can draw our strength in order to endure to the end.

2

Unlocking the Garden Gate

"If anyone would come after me, let him deny himself and take up his cross and follow me."

MATTHEW 16:24

Like most people, when I think about the Garden of Gethsemane, I think about the cross. It was, after all, the sacrifice of Jesus on the cross that brought us salvation, right? Yes, the cross was the finality of his sacrifice, and that is where he actually bore our sins and won our forgiveness. But the choices and sacrifices he made in the Garden of Gethsemane were precursors to the cross; it was there that the expulsion of blood began, and it was on the cross where it ended.

How do the events that occurred the day of his arrest connect with the finality of his sacrifice? Why did Jesus choose the Garden of Gethsemane as the place to suffer in prayer as opposed to various other religious sites? What was it that prompted him, after a long day filled with walking, preparing for the Passover, hosting the Last Supper, washing the disciples' feet, and engaging in extensive prayer, prophecy, and teaching, to choose this specific day as the one that would lead to his arrest, a sleepless night, and ultimately his crucifixion? Answers to these questions unlock the garden gate that leads us to a fuller understanding of both sorrow and joy in our own lives through the example of Jesus Christ.

Jesus' agony in the Garden of Gethsemane was far more than an event that led to the cross. Understanding what occurred the day of

Christ's arrest and grasping the symbolic nature of Gethsemane's location and surroundings will release the healing balm of Christ's sacrifice into our brokenness. And this will bring peace, joy, understanding, and restoration to our pain and anguish. On that day in the Garden of Gethsemane Jesus' own life, judging by external evidence alone, in the eyes of the eleven, had no hope. He had done many miracles, had taught the disciples so much truth, and had shown compassion to the oppressed and disabled, but now his death was imminent. I know of no one who hasn't personally faced what appeared to be an insurmountable and hopeless situation at some point in his or her life. Consider for a moment how the disciples felt when Jesus was arrested and about to be crucified.

To the disciples, Jesus' death would be the end of life as they knew it in several ways. First, they had given up their lifelong careers to follow him for the previous three years. What would they do for a living after they had switched careers in midlife and committed themselves to a ministry that now appeared to be ending? Was what they had been sharing with others merely wishful thinking? Was it all a hoax? How would they explain Jesus' death after he had done so many miracles and even raised some from the dead? Who were they now? They had gone from disciples of God to . . . what?

The second thing to consider is the physical risk the disciples would face. Jesus would soon die, and they might lose their lives as followers of the executed King of the Jews. They would witness their Lord's betrayal by Judas and would see that the Romans could be persuaded to exact the death penalty, as in the crucifixion of Jesus. They would know that the same leaders who killed Jesus would want to destroy them in an attempt to eliminate the truth, to try to show that Jesus was a fraud, and to extinguish their own raging jealousy.

Finally, Jesus had not only been their Messiah and Lord but also their friend, companion, comfort, support, encouragement, and security as they boldly ventured into ministry using their particular spiritual gifts. They had invested their most sacred and intimate selves with him, sharing all their possessions, hopes, and dreams. Suddenly their investment became not only threatened but potentially even shattered. The death of their Lord would disrupt their lives in a way that seemed irreparable.

Unlike us, the disciples did not have the New Testament to continually reassure themselves and one another that there was hope—though they should have known since Jesus had told them so from the beginning of his ministry. Sometimes during tragedy all we know to be true suddenly becomes a blur, and we begin to question what we once believed wholeheartedly. Such was the case with these men. After Jesus' arrest, they fled from his side out of fear. They lost hope, lied, denied him, doubted their faith, and mourned their future. Further, after Jesus had risen from the dead, which he had prophesied he would do, they still doubted and were shocked, surprised, alarmed, and even suspicious. When Jesus appeared to them in Galilee, they were hiding behind locked doors, fearing for their lives! Do these sound like men who believed they had hope?

I used to jokingly refer to the twelve disciples as "the twelve stooges" because some of the things they said and did seemed so out of character for godly men who had dwelled in the presence of our Savior twenty-four hours a day for over three years. How could they *not* know there was hope? But I know the end of the story, that three days later brought a drastically different outcome from the one they were personally experiencing. I have a different understanding of the events they were facing because I know how the story ends. Their faith faltered in the midst of a tragedy on which I have based my entire faith. From their shortsighted perspective, they had lost everything—at least until Jesus personally appeared, spoke, and proved himself to them.

Jesus experienced a similar crisis in the Garden of Gethsemane. Though fully God, he was also fully man, and thus the imminent terrors of the cross caused him great anguish. From an earthly perspective, it makes no logical sense that he should suffer for someone else's actions, does it? This is especially so since he was totally innocent, pure, and completely without sin. If Jesus had only focused on the anguish he was experiencing at that moment and time, we truly would have no hope because he would not have gone to the cross. Thankfully, that isn't where the story ends. Jesus focused on the spiritual component—obedience to his Father—and thus brought us hope.

Have you ever felt the way the disciples did, as though life had ended for you because of some trauma? Have you ever thought that life just can't go on? Have you ever experienced a wound so deep that even taking a simple breath, something that is God-given and natural, took a conscious effort and was difficult at best? Perhaps it was the loss of a loved one, a sudden depletion of finances, finding out your mate committed adultery, a divorce, being forced to leave your home, experiencing your mate being sent to prison, a friend's betrayal, or your child's death.

These tragedies, like many others, are Gethsemane experiences and can be the precursor to the kind of anguish that threatens to take your breath away if you even consider letting loose of the thread of faith that connects you to God. A Gethsemane experience breeds the kind of pain that comes from enduring a wound so deep that you know that the healing of it will be more painful than the tragedy that caused it. It means wrestling with such intense agony that you wake up only long enough to cry yourself back to sleep. It's those moments when you beg God to reverse the situation that led to your loss and are forced to face the fact that he won't. It's begging him relentlessly to take this cup from you, all the while knowing it's his will that you drink from it. It breeds the kind of pain that makes you not want to go on, but you know that the only other choice is to die—and at times you want just that. Gethsemanes are those times in life when you realize that you have become unwittingly intimate with misery, anguish, distress, woe, and heart-wrenching grief and fear.

Whatever the circumstance, your life has suddenly and brutally come to a stop, and you can't imagine how you'll survive the next hour, let alone the next day, week, month, or year. Hope? You think, *There is no hope.*

I've been through many Gethsemane situations during my life that bred hopelessness, despair, and agony. Looking back, my life (not to mention my emotions) seemed to be whirling out of control, and there seemed to be no reason to go on. I didn't have hope—but I also didn't have the rest of the story. I cannot tell you how many times God spared me from death at my own hand as an unbeliever. But he knew the entire story of my life—that one day I'd become his child and counsel others who felt the same despair I once endured, that I'd write books that would encourage and challenge sufferers not to lose their vision but to go on. He knew I'd have two children who would watch their mother transform from a broken child herself into a God-fearing Christian, and three grandchildren who would need a praying grandma. These are things I could not even comprehend during those times in my life, and things today I would not exchange for anything.

Perhaps you can relate to my desire at one time to cease the pain permanently. You're experiencing your own private Gethsemane. The rain is falling, the sky is dark, and visibility is slim. You're so caught up in the whirlwind of pain that you don't know which way to turn or what path to take. Death (in one way or another) seems imminent, and the anguish that you are experiencing is overwhelming. You want to bring an end to the pain. Jesus felt the same way. Matthew 26:38 tells us that he said, "My soul is very sorrowful, even to death."

Jesus understands your pain and despair. This is a silver lining—a promise from God. He's saying, "I will not leave you or forsake you. Call on me. I will answer you when you call on me with all your heart. I have a plan for you, a plan to bless you and to prosper you, to give you a hope and a future. Do not despair, for I am with you always."

Look at your pain and see your circumstance from God's perspective. *There is more to your story.* A new chapter in the Book of Life awaits your choice. Will you falter like the disciples and drown in your sorrows, or will you keep moving toward the prize, even when you can't see it clearly? As I once did, you may be asking, "But how do I get there from here? How do I go from agony to joy, from pain to praise, from confusion to clarity, from hopelessness to hope?"

Venture with me into the Garden of Gethsemane, where the scales of unbelief will be removed from your heart and where the Holy Spirit will be your guide, teacher, and companion. Our journey to freedom in Christ begins in a small garden outside Jerusalem.

3

LOCATION, LOCATION, LOCATION

And every day he was teaching in the temple, but at night he went out and lodged on the mount called Olivet.

LUKE 21:37

The most important aspect to any real estate investment is location. The precise location of a piece of land can increase or decrease the value of the property. It is said that when a Wal-Mart is built, the property around it becomes worth fifty times its original value. Jesus too thought location was important, choosing specific sites to symbolize different points he longed to make to his followers for generations to come. The Mount of Olives, the Garden of Gethsemane, and Jerusalem were all strategic in the life and death of Jesus and also have a direct correlation and meaning to the church of Christ and the suffering we endure on earth.

THE MOUNT OF OLIVES

The Mount of Olives retains great symbolism and value in relation to Jesus and his sacrificial ministry when looked at from a spiritual perspective. That was where Jesus chose to stand when he mourned and wept over Jerusalem and where he sat with his disciples as he told them of the wondrous events yet to come, of the future destruction of the Holy City, and of the sufferings and persecution that awaited him. That is also where the final triumph of his followers will occur when their Savior returns to earth someday (Matthew 24:30-31). His prophecies of the apocalyptic fall of Jerusalem were delivered on that mount (Matthew

24:1ff.; Mark 13:1ff.), and Zechariah 14:3-4 prophesies that on this site the Lord will take his stand in the "day of battle," otherwise known as the Second Coming, and will gain victory by supernaturally intervening to deliver his people from their enemies. As we can see, the Mount of Olives is no ordinary place.

As its name suggests, the hillsides of the Mount of Olives were once thick with olive groves. The trees were later cut down by the Romans to make weapons when they ransacked the city. Like the city of Jerusalem, the Mount has been of great interest to Jews for thousands of years because of its location. When standing on the Mount of Olives, the view of the city of Jerusalem is superb. Like all property with a view, this in itself makes the Mount of Olives premium land.

The Mount of Olives is located east of Jerusalem, not far beyond the Kidron Valley, about two hundred feet above the city (Matthew 21:1; 26:30; Mark 13:3; 14:26; Luke 19:37; John 18:1). Historically, this mount has been seen as a symbol of division or separation in Scripture. One example of this is Christ's return at the Second Coming as noted in Zechariah 14:4:

> On that day his feet shall stand on the Mount of Olives that lies before Jerusalem on the east, and the Mount of Olives shall be split in two from east to west by a very wide valley, so that one half of the Mount shall move northward, and the other half southward.

Here we see Jesus drawing the proverbial line of separation in the sand. The splitting of the Mount of Olives illustrates the division between those who accept him as their Savior and those who do not.

The theme of division can also be seen in issues of spiritual allegiance. Prior to Jesus' death on the cross, sacrifices had to be made for the sins of God's people again and again, pointing forward to Jesus' sacrifice for us. The southern end of the Mount of Olives was the place ordained by God in Old Testament times for this spiritual purification of his people. It was chosen to be the location where the high priest slaughtered and burned the sacrificial cow (compare 2 Kings 23:4) and the place where the Israelites worshiped God (2 Samuel 15:30-32). Contrary to its original godly sacrifices, it later became the location where King

Solomon built "high places" for the goddess Ashtoreth and the false god Moab (compare Judges 2:13; 1 Samuel 7:4). Thus, the people departed from God and joined themselves to idols. As a result of their spiritual adultery, the Mount of Olives became associated with the departure of the visible manifestation of God's glory from the Temple, signifying Israel's imminent expulsion from the land (Ezekiel 10:18; 11:23).

Other significant stories in the Bible further support the ongoing decisive theme of the Mount of Olives. One of these occurred when Absalom rebelled against his father, King David. Absalom sought to rule in place of his father, and as his army marched into Jerusalem, the dethroned king fled the city, his feet bare and his head covered in shame as he grappled with overwhelming sorrow and despair. As he stood on the Mount of Olives, he wept over his son's choice to betray him and turned to God for help (2 Samuel 15:30-32).

In respect to the day Jesus was arrested, we see the theme of division and separation most clearly in Matthew 26:30-31:

> And when they had sung a hymn, they went out to the Mount of Olives. Then Jesus said to them, "You will all fall away because of me this night. For it is written, 'I will strike the shepherd, and the sheep of the flock will be scattered.'"

As we walk a little farther onto the Mount, we find a sacred garden, further supporting the theme of division and opening more doors to understanding Jesus' choice of refuge. Its name is Gethsemane.

THE GARDEN OF GETHSEMANE

Although the Mount of Olives in its entirety is of great spiritual worth, it's the Garden of Gethsemane, wherein lies a small but influential cemetery, that Jews in Jerusalem see as having the most value. It is believed by some that when Jesus Christ returns and all the dead are resurrected, the people who are buried on the Mount of Olives will be the first to rise from the dead.

In the Garden of Eden, the first Adam fell by yielding to temptation, causing humanity to fall into sinful ruin and to progressively deteriorate.

In the Garden of Gethsemane, the "last Adam" (1 Corinthians 15:45) faced the same choice but did not fall. To fully understand the options before Jesus and indirectly before us, we need to take a historical walk through the Garden of Gethsemane.

Luke 21:37 is one of many Scriptures that tell us that after Jesus spent the day ministering, he would spend the night in the Garden of Gethsemane. The multitude of olive trees, the dense foliage, and the cool evening breezes no doubt provided a sanctuary of rest for our King. We all have a place we prefer to go above all others that brings us comfort after dealing with the demands of a hectic day and the relentless onslaughts of the world. For me, it would have likely been the Sea of Galilee at sunrise or sunset. But Gethsemane was Jesus' place of refuge. There Jesus spent time meditating, praying, and resting his body from the labors of the day.

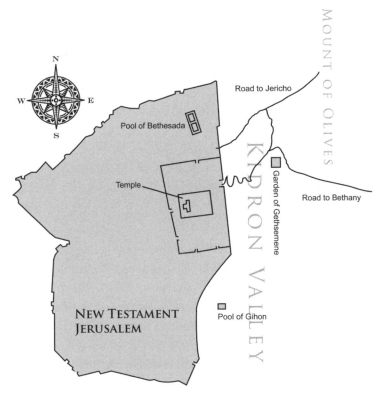

The name *Gethsemane* is derived from the Hebrew expression *Gat Shemen*, which means "a press for crushing olives." Although its name is in direct correlation to the natural abundance of olive trees in the region and to the olive press located in the Garden, the association between the crushing of the resilient fruit and the crushing of our Savior's spirit in the Garden cannot go unnoticed. Nor can we ignore the obvious correlation of the crushing of our own fragile humanity when grief consumes us. The agonizing paradox for us is that while we feel as though we are dying internally, externally we must go on living. The coexistence of life and death brings confusion, agony, and defeat to the one experiencing such torment.

The Garden of Gethsemane was located east of Jerusalem on the most southern part of the Mount of Olives. Between the Garden and Jerusalem lies the Kidron Valley, horizontally spanning the entire eastern part of the city. The Kidron Valley runs between the east wall of Jerusalem along the Temple Mount and the Mount of Olives and extends through the Judean desert. The valley is only twenty miles long but has a descent of 3,912 feet, and thus the waters that run through it during the wet season are often described as torrential and rapid. The Bible informs us that the Kidron Valley was the location where King Asa destroyed and burned his grandmother's idol (1 Kings 15:13), where Athaliah was executed (2 Kings 11:16), and where, in its plush fields, King Josiah had Hilkiah the High Priest destroy all the equipment used in the worship of the pagan god Baal (2 Kings 23:4). After King Josiah had the idols destroyed, the Kidron Valley became the receptacle for the impurities and abominations of idol worship when removed from the Temple and destroyed by the adherents of Jehovah (2 Kings 23:4, 6, 12; 2 Chronicles 29:16; 30:14). Also, in the time of Josiah, this valley was the common cemetery of Jerusalem (2 Kings 23:6; Jeremiah 26:23; 31:40).

The name *Kidron* actually means "gloomy" or "dark," and this gorge was referred to as "The Valley of the Shadow of Death" for two reasons. First, at sunrise it was overshadowed by the cemetery on the Mount of Olives at the Garden at Gethsemane; and, second, during Sukkoth, the feast of temporary booths, four huge lampposts were erected in the Temple courts of Jerusalem that lit up the entire town—except this valley.

While Psalm 23 is often read during a funeral, biblically "the shadow of death" represents deep darkness and blackness, not necessarily physical death. It refers to God's leading his people safely through a difficult situation, no matter how dark or threatening it may be. Those who are agonizing over the loss of a loved one or are facing deep disappointment regarding the current state of their life are assured that the darkest night will not consume them if they allow God to guide them.

The Kidron Valley is an important section of the road of anguish and healing that we find ourselves traveling. South of the Mount of Olives and southeast of Jerusalem was a natural spring of water referred to as the Pool of Gihon. This pool or spring rose outside the city walls on the west bank as a brook that ran through the Kidron Valley and served as the main water source for Jerusalem. It was at the Pool of Gihon where King Hezekiah built a tunnel that let water flow undetected into the city of Jerusalem as preparation for the Assyrian siege. In order to prevent the besiegers from finding water, Hezekiah "closed the upper outlet of the waters of Gihon and directed them down to the west side of the city of David" (2 Chronicles 32:30; compare 33:14). The tunnel was approximately 1,750 feet in length and still exists in modern Jerusalem.

The name *Gihon* means "conduit"—that is, a means to get from Point A to Point B. It also means "spring" or "pool." The importance and significance of the location and meaning of the Pool of Gihon is astonishing. The first thing we must consider is that the Pool of Gihon is a conduit for natural spring water to travel through the Kidron Valley— that is, the Valley of the Shadow of Death—into Jerusalem. Similarly, Jesus is our conduit, the means for us to get from where we currently are—in a state of brokenness—to a place of healing or wholeness. Further, he is referred to as Living Water, haveing no impurities. In looking at those similarities, we must consider that both the Pool of Gihon and Jesus are conduits for water. The difference is that one gives liquid that will quench a physical thirst, and the other provides living water that will leave the one who partakes of it thirsting no more (John 4:10, 14).

Apart from the fact that Jesus is the Living Water that runs through our spiritual veins, water has historically been seen in the Bible as a way of representing God's action. It is used in the Bible as a homestead for life

(Genesis 1:21), for nourishment (Genesis 2:6), to cleanse evil (Genesis 7:7), as a refuge (Exodus 2:10), as a conduit for miracles (Exodus 7:17; 14:28; Matthew 14:25), to fulfill a promise of provision (Exodus 17:6), to cleanse and purify (Leviticus 1:9), as a holy instrument (Numbers 5:17), for repentance (Matthew 3:11), as a blessing, and more. Who can forget the lesson given to us by Jesus, the servant-leader, who washed his disciples' feet the night before he was arrested to demonstrate the humility found in true leadership (John 13).

Not so ironically, water is the one substance that is essential to humanity's survival. Equally so, the Living Water—that is, Jesus—is essential for spiritual survival. The message is clear: we cannot walk through the Valley of the Shadow of Death without partaking of the Living Water. Without him, we would become dehydrated in the midst of the desert we are walking through and would shrivel up and die. Equally important is the fact that in order to get from where we currently reside in the midst of our anguish, we must go *through* the Valley of the Shadow of Death to reach the place where freedom, healing, and restoration was won—the Garden of Gethsemane.

North of the Pool of Gihon is a hill that rises about 150 feet higher than Jerusalem. Near the base of that hill is the Garden of Gethsemane. That Garden is situated at an angle off Jericho Road where the road splits into two branches, once again supporting the already existing theme of division outlined earlier regarding the Mount of Olives. One road leads directly up the face of the Mount of Olives and then winds gently around the southern brow of the hill and leads to Jericho. The other leads to Bethany. This crossroad meant that every traveler had to make a choice at the Garden to either go toward Jericho or Bethany. At first glance this split in the road and the choice it creates and the location of the Garden is not symbolic. However, with a closer look into the Bible, which explains the meaning of these roads, we begin to see a bigger picture.

Jericho Road was a twenty-mile, treacherous, winding road that descended from Jerusalem through barren hills toward the Jordan River just north of the Dead Sea. To make this road even more difficult to travel on, Jerusalem is 2,500 feet *above* sea level, and Jericho is 1,200 feet *below* sea level. That's a drop of 3,700 feet in a very short span. In biblical times,

Jericho Road was not so fondly referred to as "The Way of Blood" because of the dangers that it posed.

In Jesus' time, thieves and criminals would escape Jerusalem by going past the Mount of Olives and over its towering mountains toward Jericho. Once over these challenges, they entered a high desert region where rocks and sand abounded and food, water, and life-sustaining resources were scarce. As a result, groups of bandits would work together to overtake unprotected travelers. We see confirmation of the dangers of this road in the Parable of the Good Samaritan, in which Jesus' protagonist took a man who was stripped, assaulted, brutally beaten, robbed, and left grasping for life and cared for him (Luke 10:25-37).

Consider Jericho Road in relation to your current or recent state of agony. If you are walking on this road, you are choosing to walk alone. "The Way of Blood" is dangerous and life-threatening, and if you live through it, you will nevertheless have grave memories and scars. You are not sacrificing the blood of Jesus on this road of self-pity and self-accomplishment but your own. After all, you are walking it by your own choice. It is an exceedingly hard road to travel upon—emotionally, mentally, physically, and especially spiritually. God may, like the Good Samaritan, intervene, sending others to walk with you and to help wrap your wounds. But your injuries will never be completely healed until you submit them to the Great Healer for the balm of Gilead that only he can provide.

I traveled Jericho Road many times in my life before I was a Christian, and even a couple of times after giving my heart to Jesus. I began to receive secular counseling when I was seventeen, studied psychology in school, read every self-help book I could get my hands on, and attended thousands of hours' worth of workshops to work through the pain and anguish that came from years of abuse as a child. In doing so I received a certain level of healing in my life, but never *complete* healing because God never intended for those tools to heal me. They were merely Band-Aids that covered the wounds so that the impact of life against my injuries was not so blunt. I ended up functioning in a somewhat healthy manner in life, but I always retained scars and was haunted by chronic depression and endless memories that continually told me I was worthless and unlovable.

The other choice one could make at the Garden of Gethsemane was to forsake going to Jericho via "The Way of Blood" and instead go approximately two miles from Jerusalem to Bethany, a place Jesus visited often. In Bible times there were such large groves of date palms around the perennial spring within Jericho that the town was often called "The City of Palm Trees." The name Bethany, on the other hand, meant "house of affliction, depression, or misery." It was here that Jesus raised Lazarus from the dead and where Jesus was approached by Mary with an alabaster vial of costly perfume to anoint him for burial. Additionally, Bethany is the location where our Savior would make his triumphal entry (Mark 11:1).

Interestingly enough, Jesus stayed with friends in "the house of affliction, depression, or misery" the last six days before his crucifixion. Every morning he would journey to Jerusalem and then return to Bethany in the evening. It was along this journey during this week that Jesus cursed the fig tree that was full of leaves but was barren. The fig tree served as an emblem of the Jewish nation, and this act of cursing the tree served as a symbol of God's coming judgment on the Jewish leaders who were opposing him. Ironically, the biblical symbolism of the fig tree is one of choice—peace and blessing or selfishness and cruelty.

Just as we examined Jericho Road and its meaning in relation to our suffering, we must look honestly at the road to Bethany. No one would willingly visit a home referred to as the "house of affliction, depression, or misery," let alone take up residence there. That would be a house I'd avoid at all costs. But Jesus willingly went there for our sake. And we are called to go there for his sake (2 Timothy 3:12). We are told that just as Jesus won our pardon and overcame the world through his suffering, we can be victorious through his grace and strength (Matthew 5:11-12).

The road to Bethany is not one we take alone, nor one that has not been taken previously by our Savior. He walked that road daily for a week before the day of his death. He has walked down that road, and he promised to walk down it with us, never at any moment leaving or forsaking us along the way. The road to Bethany does not keep us from experiencing pain and heartache, but it does hold the promise that our ever-present Companion will give us all the grace and strength we need to get to our destination as we choose to walk with him. The icing on the cake is that when we get to the other side, we will do so without residual scars, depression, regret, or self-pity. Jesus was not known for healing people partially but completely, 100 percent, and he replaces our past pain with a peace that surpasses all understanding.

As we look at the map of our life in all aspects—the past, the present, and the direction in which we are headed—we will see that we've spent our life seeking peace—especially from the results of sin in our lives. If you were sexually abused as a child, you live with inner chaos as you grapple with the anguish of someone else's violation of your innocence. Equally so, if you sin against another, you live with internal chaos because you cannot reconcile your actions to what you know to be true—God's Word. The cycle of sin creates inner turmoil whether you are the receiver or the giver. Because of our inner anguish, we seek tranquillity. The many twelve-step groups today prove our longing search for peace.

First we seek peace from the void inside us. Then we spend the rest of our lives searching for tranquillity despite life's everyday heartache and pain, serenity in the midst of trials and tribulations, and peace during suffering. And this is not in vain if we go to Jesus for fulfillment. Isaiah 53:5 tells us that Jesus' death on the cross was for our iniquities ("he was wounded for our transgressions; he was crushed for our iniquities"), our peace ("upon him was the chastisement that brought us peace"), and our sickness ("with his stripes we are healed"). In other words, one of the reasons Jesus died was so we could have peace with God. Reconciliation with God through faith in Jesus Christ brings peace, and we become reconciled with God when we confess our sinfulness and receive his pardon through Jesus Christ. He then enables us to forgive others and turn our suffering over to him. In other words, internal peace with God brings external peace with our circumstances.

We must come to understand that when God created us, he put within us an innate craving for peace, a by-product of wholeness that we can attain only through him. His desire and vision for us is that we would walk in peace despite our circumstances. As we move into the symbolism behind the city of Jerusalem, we will come to a better understanding of this desire of God for us.

JERUSALEM

Jerusalem was the capital of the ancient kingdom of Israel. The city is situated on an uneven rocky plateau at an elevation of about 2,500 feet. It is surrounded on three sides by deep and precipitous ravines created by three instrumental valleys—the Kidron, Tyropoen, and Hinnom. In respect to location, one of the major selling points of this city is that it is located about fourteen miles from the Dead Sea and thirty-three miles east of the Mediterranean and stands on the edge of one of the highest tablelands in Palestine. Its location has helped give it prestige and protection for thousands of years.

During the time of Jesus, Jerusalem was predominantly a small, isolated fortress, valued more for its location than for its beauty or size. However, the city was also known for its great splendor. Psalm 48:2 poetically referred to Jerusalem as "beautiful in elevation . . . the joy of all the earth." Lamentations fondly calls the city "the perfection of beauty" and "the joy of all the earth" (2:15).

Jerusalem is the place where Jesus' identity was first confirmed to his parents and indirectly to the existing Christian church. When our Savior was only eight days old, Joseph and Mary took him to Jerusalem to present him to the Lord (as commanded in the Law of the Lord—every firstborn male was to be consecrated to the Lord) and to offer a sacrifice on behalf of his birth. At that time Simeon proclaimed his exhilaration and joy over seeing his Savior and prophesied the falling and rising of many in Israel. Additionally, he blessed Joseph and Mary and prophesied to Mary that she would suffer because of her Son's sacrifice for all humanity, saying, "And a sword will pierce through your own soul also" (Luke 2:25-35). The temple prophetess, Anna, also confirmed to Jesus' parents and to those looking forward to the coming of the Messiah that Jesus had been born to redeem Jerusalem (vv. 36-38).

We see Jesus' ministry manifesting itself in Jerusalem for the first time when he was twelve, attending the Feast of the Passover with his parents. After the feast was completed and his parents had begun their trip home and realized he was not with their traveling company, they found him in the temple courts, sitting among the teachers, listening to them and asking them questions (Luke 2:41-51). So Jerusalem was a place of proclaiming the identity of the King of kings to the world, and also a place where truth would be proclaimed by our Savior that would separate the goats from the sheep. Jerusalem was, of course, also the place where Jesus was crucified as he bore our sins and brought us salvation. As we read the Bible we find that Jerusalem was in all aspects the place where Jesus' ministry began and ended.

Over the millennia, many names and meanings have been given to the city of Jerusalem. In the book of Genesis, the city is referred to as Salem or Shalem, and its name means "peace." The name Melchizedek, King of Salem, means "righteous king." Other names and meanings include but are not limited to:

- Moriah—"chosen of the Lord"
- Jebus—"threshing floor" or "trodden down"
- Ariel—"Lion of God"
- Al-Quds—"The Noble Holy Place"

As you can see by its meanings, Jerusalem clearly represents what we know through the Bible to be true. Jesus, the Righteous King who is the Lord chosen by our Creator and Father in heaven, was trodden down for us (Psalm 72:1; Isaiah 43:10; Mark 8:31). He is the Lion of God, and because of his spiritual lineage, his death for our sins, and the events yet to transpire in and around Jerusalem during the Second Coming, Jesus has made the city a noble and holy place (Revelation 5:5). Knowing the events that transpired in Jerusalem, we can see how the city's name reflects its mission and purpose. But the Bible intimately associates Jerusalem with another crucial reality that those of us who are in the midst of suffering will find very important—a vision of peace.

When we are in the midst of suffering, peace is generally consumed with the whys, what-ifs, and if onlys. The serenity we obtained through the Holy Spirit at conversion is replaced with what we call our "right" to be angry and disappointed in God due to our circumstances. But that is not the way it has to be, nor the way God designed it to be. As a matter of fact, it's his desire and vision for us to have tranquillity—that is, to retain an inner peace that surpasses all understanding even though the world is spinning out of control around us. It is not only feasible but possible to stand on solid ground in an unstable land during an earthquake, to be in the midst of a raging fire and be untouched by the flames, to be in a torrential rain and not get wet. What the world says is impossible, God says is possible through him.

You see, Jerusalem is a metaphor for a perfected world, a picture of eternal life, which is attainable now in large measure, though not perfectly, as we walk with Christ. It is a vision of peace that is within reach, available, and accessible for believers whenever they choose to cling to him. This vision of peace is one of promise: if we hold on to his promises, the Prince of Peace will be with us and will comfort, teach, and guide us.

Let me assure you that you stand at a crucial crossroads in your healing in the midst of difficult circumstances, and your choice will inevitably determine your outcome. I've stood at this crossroads before and willingly chose Jericho Road. I could see God's vision of peace for me within grasp, but I falsely believed that I didn't need God's help and could make it on my own. But my best-laid plans and attempts at healing and restoration in life took me to a place of further slavery and deterioration where healing was minimal and sanity questionable and where death looked unavoidable. I ended up taking the road to Bethany only after crawling down Jericho Road for a while. The difference has been life-changing.

If you dare forsake yourself and your ways and cling to God, you too will experience healing, freedom, and joy in the midst of misery, depression, and affliction. This is not an easy road to travel but one you *must* journey down, for you cannot stand forever at the crossroads lest you drown alone in your sorrows. If you choose to journey down Jericho Road, you may arrive at the road to Bethany at another time, but a crucial part of who you are will be stripped, assaulted, brutally beaten, robbed, and left grasping for life, for the Jericho Road is the way of self, and self has no ability to stimulate or create joy, peace, healing, or restoration or to breathe life into your lifeless soul.

4

The Calm Before the Storm

"Go into the city to a certain man and say to him, 'The Teacher says, My time is at hand. I will keep the Passover at your house with my disciples.'"

MATTHEW 26:48

On June 20, 2001, Andrea Yates, with a vacant stare, confessed to police that she had just methodically drowned each of her five children, ages six months to seven years. Shortly after that fateful day I sat with Andrea's husband, Russell, and discussed the tragedy of his children's deaths with him. Although it seemed evident that he was grieving, I saw a peace within Russell that surpassed any understanding I could comprehend or imagine from a parental point of view. I reasoned God out of the inner tranquillity that I saw in Russell's eyes, and from my experience as a counselor and from an educational perspective I told myself that he was in shock, that in order to survive he had emotionally detached from the horrific events of that fateful day. I wouldn't have blamed him if that were truly the case. But since that time Russell and I have spent many hours talking over the phone and in person, and I've seen a faith in God that can only be compared to that of Job.

According to Russell, the day Andrea murdered her five children was just an ordinary day. She fixed the kids breakfast and put lip balm on a son's mouth at his request. Knowing that Russell would leave for work around 8 and that her mother-in-law would come to help her with the kids around 10, Andrea gave the kids something to do while she went into the bathroom and filled the bathtub with water to implement the plan the psychotic voices in her mind were instructing her to carry out. Although she was mentally ill and had been on medication for years, there were no red flags, abnormal behavior, or other indication that this day would be any different from the many that had preceded it.

As an engineer for NASA, Russell drove thirty minutes across town to work on the space shuttle like he had every other day for the last several years. When he left home that morning, he had attained what most Americans consider the perfect life—a wife, children, an upper-middle-class home in the suburbs, and a solid future with a high-profile company. But when he returned home an hour and a half later, his entire life and dreams for his future had been shattered.

Most of the time we can look back and see, preceding an event that caused our suffering, a time when things were in order, serene, and going smoothly, perhaps promising a great future. Maybe the pregnancy and birth of your first child brought you much anticipation and joy, only to end as a stillbirth, or perhaps you and your mate took a long-awaited romantic vacation only weeks before you found out your spouse had been having an affair. For nineteen-year-old Sue (not her real name) acceptance to an Ivy League college promised a great future but ended in a rape during her first semester of school. For Laurie and Jason (also not their real names) his long-awaited retirement promised to fulfill their lifelong dream to travel across America together. Their hopes were destroyed when they found out that Laurie had less than six months to live. Without a hint of its presence, cancer had been spreading and consuming her body for months.

Such a calm before the storm is usually identified as a time when life appears to be at its best and there is no hint of the catastrophe looming in the future. For Russell Yates, it was the weeks and months before his family tragedy. His wife, after having four beautiful boys, had given birth to their first daughter, Mary, six months earlier. They'd purchased a home and had saved a substantial amount of money. He and Andrea were in love, and their four boys—Noah, John, Paul, and Luke—were healthy and happy. Life was at its peak for them, and it was easy to feel as though they were flying above the radar of tragedy. But that was not the case.

Calamity not only came calling without an invitation or announcement as far as Russell could see. It came like a thief in the night and stole, killed, and destroyed everything and anything that was precious to Russell. In less than ninety minutes his beautiful family was gone—permanently.

For the disciples, the calm before the storm occurred during the days and hours preceding the Passover Supper, the yearly meal that commemorated the release of the Jews from centuries of slavery in Egypt long ago. They had spent the week traveling back and forth between Bethany and Jerusalem, watching Jesus do miracles and sharing the message of good news, the same activities they'd been doing for three years without incident. Nothing out of the ordinary had occurred on the day of Passover. Jesus prayed, did miracles, and taught the people through parables, all of which he'd done since his ministry began. He had washed the disciples' feet, and though that was unique, it was certainly not out of character for the servant-King. Even the preparations for the Passover Supper weren't out of the ordinary. The accommodations had been made at Jesus' request, and all fell into place just like he said they would.

Jesus had talked about his upcoming sacrifice and death. As they walked up to Jerusalem to celebrate the Passover he told them, "See, we are going up to Jerusalem, and everything that is written about the Son of Man by the prophets will be accomplished" (Luke 18:31). He even got specific with them. "The Son of Man will be delivered over to the chief priests and the scribes, and they will condemn him to death and deliver him over to the Gentiles. And they will mock him and spit on him, and flog him and kill him" (Mark 10:33-34). But the disciples did not understand any of what he was saying. Luke 18:34 tells us that the meaning of Jesus' words was "hidden from them." And because of this, they didn't ask for clarification, didn't anticipate tragedy, didn't prepare themselves by strengthening their hearts through prayer, felt no fear, and did not wrestle with the anxiety of what would happen to them and their own ministries should his words become a reality in the immediate future.

As the disciples prepared for the Passover meal, they were blissfully unaware that Jesus, the Lamb of God who partook of the annual ceremony with them, would himself be sacrificed in the days to follow or that within hours everything they knew to be real and true would suddenly become questionable to them. All they knew for certain was what was about to occur according to *their* plans—the Passover meal.

Such is the case with most believers. Scripture tells us that we will suffer, go through trials and tribulations, and experience heartache and grief. We should *expect* to suffer in life because of sin—our own and that of others. It's inevitable. Sin is infectious and wounds everyone and everything it touches. As I said in my previous books *Engaging the Enemy* and *A Parents' Guide to Spiritual Warfare*, wounded people wound people, and because we are all wounded by sin (our own and others'), we inevitably sin against others, causing even more wounds. This is a vicious but true cycle of spiritual defeat that originated in the Garden of Eden.

Jesus spoke frankly to his disciples concerning their future, and he has done so with us as well. He taught in unmistakable language that following him means bearing a cross and drinking a cup of suffering (see, for example, Luke 9:23). Jesus has told us that we will be hated by the enemy of our souls, by the world, and sometimes even by those who are closest to us—our friends and family. He even told us that some will persecute us, believing they are doing a great service to God (John 16:2). Yet, like the disciples, it sometimes seems as if his words are hidden from us. So we do not prepare our spirits for the natural consequences of sin, the onslaughts of the enemy, our spirit's battles with the flesh, or the attacks from the world. As a result, we often approach our suffering like the disciples may have approached that Passover, as if it is just something that has to be done, not really understanding that we have a choice, not grasping that although we cannot control the cause of our suffering, we can prepare and control how we will handle the effects of the trauma.

Because the disciples did not heed the words of Jesus, they failed miserably in the hours that followed. We cannot afford to do the same because for some of us, suffering is a life or death issue. We must understand what the particular situation is about and must handle it appropriately or we will also fail when, like the disciples, our faith is tested and our loyalty is pushed to the breaking point. We want to know why we suffer, and although God might not give us the full answer (just as he chose not to do with Job), we will have increased understanding as we grasp the meaning of the Passover meal and the Lord's Supper preceding our Savior's suffering.

THE SIGNIFICANCE OF THE PASSOVER MEAL

Jesus told his disciples, "I have earnestly desired to eat this Passover with you before I suffer" (Luke 22:15).

The Passover commemorates the Exodus, observing the day that God saved the Israelites from slavery in Egypt. But the symbolism behind the Passover meal went far beyond that momentous deliverance and would prove to have a depth of meaning that even the disciples didn't truly understand fifteen hundred years later when they met with Jesus in a secluded room in Jerusalem to celebrate this historical event.

When God implements a plan, it never has only immediate meaning and effect. When the Creator of the universe puts an idea into motion, he has eternity in mind. He interweaves the same intention or theme in multiple ways throughout humanity and throughout the ages, thus offering the fulfillment of his promises for all who come to him in faith.

When God instructed the Israelites to slay a lamb and place its blood around their doors as protection from the plague of death that would move through Egypt, he was also thinking of the millions of people he had created and would create and how their sin would lead to death and separation from him. Even more relevant for our current topic of suffering, he was considering *you* and the anguish you would be experiencing at such a time as this. Let me explain.

After slaying the lamb and placing its blood around their doorposts, as directed by God, the Israelites were to eat all of the lamb they had slaughtered. They were instructed to do so to strengthen and prepare themselves for their march from Egypt where they had been held in captivity for centuries. We cannot ignore the symbolism between these commands to the Israelites to allow God to save them from slavery and death and to fortify themselves for a journey and that of Jesus for his disciples and the church to partake of the bread (representing his flesh) and to drink from the cup (representing his blood) for the same *spiritual* purposes. Jesus is our Passover Lamb (1 Corinthians 5:7). For those followers of Christ who are suffering, the symbolism behind partaking of the Lamb is grand, for doing so will strengthen and prepare them for the remainder of their journey, however long it may be.

There is another symbolic comparison between food at the Passover meal, the Israelites' deliverance from Egypt, and our own salvation. Bitter herbs were used to season the lamb, meant to remind the Israelites of their bitter slavery. To be a servant to sin and its by-product, suffering, is bitter for all. But the roasted lamb would remind them that when a lamb's blood was applied to the doorposts and when they ate of that lamb within the safety of their homes, the death angel passed over them. Equally so, when we place the blood of the Lamb on the doorposts of our hearts, the bitter sting of death (spiritual or physical) is balanced out and loses its effect.

Additionally, stewed fruit accompanied the meal. Its color and consistency were meant to be reminiscent of their making bricks for Pharaoh. By remembering their slavery and oppressive manual labor, the Israelites were meant to see that their hard work had brought no deliverance but only further slavery. There is no joy in a day filled with making bricks for a ruthless ruler. In relation to suffering, our best effort to do what we think will bring deliverance just produces further bondage and disappointment. That is because if we are not placing our pain at the foot of the cross, we are trying to endure it through our own strength. Clearly, our best work on our own behalf cannot deliver us, nor does it have the power to bring healing. We must look to our Father for freedom and deliverance. Additionally, suffering reminds us of the bitter effects of sin, which in the context of our relationship with Christ leads directly to our hope and anticipation of eternity where we will no longer experience any aspects of suffering.

God knew what was required for the liberation of his people. Jesus Christ was the true sacrifice to which every Passover lamb had been pointing for fifteen hundred years. What the death of the lamb had been to Israel in Egypt, Jesus' death would be to God's people. Jesus left his heavenly home to endure a human life on earth that would end in a horrific death in order to bring us freedom from pain and death in all aspects. To further emphasize his point, Jesus implemented an ordinance that we call the Lord's Supper, meant to remind us every time we observe it that freedom from sin and its effects are accessible if we rely on him.

THE IMPLEMENTATION OF THE LORD'S SUPPER

Our Savior knew full well what would occur in the hours following the Passover dinner with his disciples. Although he had told them of his impending death and their upcoming rejection of him, they were oblivious to the fact that on this very night they would all forsake him. Knowing the disciples would bail out on him, Jesus nevertheless graciously chose the last night before his crucifixion to bestow a parting gift of great significance to them. He did this because he knew they would suffer from his death and without spiritual intervention would not recover.

Jesus knew the disciples would not only grieve but would *suffer* over their rejection and abandonment of him—at the hand of the Jews who sought to take his life and by their own guilty consciences that would never let them forget how they had failed their most faithful friend. As a result, Jesus implemented a sacred ceremony that would be symbolic of his sacrifice on their behalf and would also strengthen and prepare them, and us, for their impending suffering as a result of sin. Luke 22:19-20 tells us the story of Jesus' implementation of the Lord's Supper:

> *And he took bread, and when he had given thanks, he broke it and gave it to them, saying, "This is my body, which is given for you. Do this in remembrance of me." And likewise the cup after they had eaten, saying, "This cup that is poured out for you is the new covenant in my blood."*

PARTAKING OF THE BREAD

While Jesus and his disciples were eating the Passover meal, our Savior took an unleavened loaf of bread, which having no yeast represented the absence of sin in his life, thanked his Father for it, broke it, distributed it, and encouraged the disciples to partake. Not so ironically, the unleavened bread was also symbolic of "the bread of affliction" because it reminded the Israelites of their persecution in Egypt (see Deuteronomy 16:3). Now during the Lord's Supper this unleavened bread was given an even greater significance—it represented Jesus' body, the breaking of his spirit, and the affliction he would endure on the cross.

By partaking of the bread, they were accepting his promise to intervene on behalf of them and their sins. Jesus' words are not found in the historical Passover meal; thus we know that he was implementing a new covenant and ritual. I'm confident that though the disciples ate the bread as Jesus instructed, they did not understand the full meaning behind their Master's request. Nor would they understand for several days to come.

Jesus distinctly told the disciples they were to partake of the bread "in remembrance of me" (Luke 22:19). Thus the Lord's Supper is not a sacrifice—it is a commemorative ordinance. The bread of which we partake during the Lord's Supper is intended to remind us of Christ's body given to die on the cross for our sins and suffering.

DRINKING OF THE CUP

In Old Testament times, out of fear that those closest to them would poison their drinks, ancient kings appointed cupbearers to sample their beverage first. Naturally, if the drink was poisoned, the cupbearer died rather than the king. Nehemiah tells us that the role of a cupbearer was a very trusted position, one that he held for King Artaxerxes (Nehemiah 1:11; 2:1). The king had to personally enjoy the presence of such a person because of necessity he was continually in the king's presence. Thus this trusted individual was influential as well and was often asked to advise the king on daily matters.

Since that time, the catch-all phrase *drinking the cup* has come to symbolize sharing the consequence of what the cup contains. An example of this is seen in Revelation 17:4 and 18:3, where we are told that the world drinks from the cup of Babylon, which is full of "abominations and . . . impurities" and "the wine of the passion of her sexual immorality." As a result, those who partake of Babylon's cup will also inherit her outcome—divine punishment resulting in spiritual death and eternal separation from God. This does not paint a pretty picture of the end times, and Revelation further shares that partaking of that cup reaps "the wine of God's wrath, poured full strength into the cup of his anger" (14:10).

God's children, however, are called to drink another cup. Psalm 116:13 tells us, "I will lift up the cup of salvation." This cup contains all the blessings of God, especially eternal life and reward in his kingdom, but it also includes sharing in the sufferings and sorrows of Jesus. The life of the apostle Paul is a proclamation of suffering in relation to the Christian's walk:

> Are they servants of Christ? I am a better one—I am talking like a madman—with far greater labors, far more imprisonments, with countless beatings, and often near death. Five times I received at the hands of the Jews the forty lashes less one. Three times I was beaten with rods. Once I was stoned. Three times I was shipwrecked; a night and a day I was adrift at sea; on frequent journeys, in danger from rivers, danger from robbers, danger from my own people, danger from Gentiles, danger in the city, danger in the wilderness, danger at sea, danger from false brothers; in toil and hardship, through many a sleepless night, in hunger and thirst, often without food, in cold and exposure. And, apart from other things, there is the daily pressure on me of my anxiety for all the churches. (2 Corinthians 11:23-28)

Paul was talking about all kinds of suffering—physical, emotional, mental, spiritual. He was suffering from the results of man's sinful nature (including his own) and from direct assaults by the enemy of his soul. But he found the strength to go on in Jesus Christ on a day-to-day basis.

One of the many things I admire about the apostle Paul is his honesty, vulnerability, and transparency regarding his walk. In 2 Corinthians 12:7-9 we see that he asked the Lord to remove from him the suffering at the hand of Satan with which he was wrestling:

> So to keep me from being too elated by the surpassing greatness of the revelations, a thorn was given me in the flesh, a messenger of Satan to harass me, to keep me from being too elated. Three times I pleaded with the Lord about this, that it should leave me. But he said to me, "My grace is sufficient for you, for my power is made perfect in weakness."

Paul tells us that he was given a "thorn" to keep him from becoming conceited. In the Lord's answer we see that the apostle did not get a complete, instantaneous healing but instead was given sufficient grace and power to deal with the anguish at hand.

The apostle Paul was a righteous man, and yet he still suffered and grappled with sin and desired the deliverance found in God alone. Our Father granted that for him on a momentary basis, saying that his grace was sufficient for his follower. Paul drank of the cup not because he wanted to endure torment but because he trusted God's answer in the gospel.

During the Last Supper Jesus took the cup and told the disciples to drink of it saying, "This cup that is poured out for you is the new covenant in my blood" (Luke 22:20). By referring to the cup as "the new covenant in my blood," Jesus was contrasting his atoning work of shedding his blood with the previous covenant when burnt offerings and young bulls were sacrificed and offered to the Lord.

In Exodus 24:6-8 we learn that everything of significance to God was doused in blood—half on the altar and the other half on the people. They all dripped with blood. That's not a pretty visual that fits nicely into a pristine box in our limited view of Christ's sacrifice, but it definitely emphasizes the seriousness of sin and shows the startling truth that the only sufficient payment for sin is death. The weakness of the Old Covenant was that it depended on man's keeping his pledge to obey the Law, which he could not do.

As the Book of the Covenant was read, the people responded in one voice, "All the words that the LORD has spoken we will do" (Exodus 24:3), but they couldn't honestly fulfill their words because of their sin nature. Thus another covenant had to be implemented—one that could be kept, one that was dependent upon another whose word and action would not falter—Jesus Christ. The New Covenant also involved an ocean of blood, but it was the blood of One who was worthy and able to fulfill God's Law and to redeem our souls.

The wine or juice in the Communion service is intended to remind us of Christ's blood shed to make atonement for our transgressions. In short, the Lord's Supper pictures the sacrifice and satisfaction made for our sin. As believers we know that just as the bread was broken, Jesus' body was broken; and just as the people of Israel associated the death of the Passover lamb with their deliverance from Egypt, so we associate Jesus' redemptive death with our deliverance from sin and its ultimate result—death. Equally so, when Jesus refers to the wine as blood that was "poured out" for us, we understand that he was referring to his physical blood that was heavily poured out for us for the purpose of our salvation.

To fully appreciate the breaking of the bread and the drinking of the cup, we need to understand that they were symbolic of the sufferings that awaited Christ on the cross as he overcame our alienation from God and thus our resulting lack of peace because of sin and its by-product, suffering. Describing Jesus' anguish, the psalmist wrote:

> *I am poured out like water,*
> *and all my bones are out of joint;*
> *my heart is like wax;*
> *it is melted within my breast;*
> *my strength is dried up like a potsherd,*
> *and my tongue sticks to my jaws;*
> *you lay me in the dust of death . . .*
> *they have pierced my hands and feet. (Psalm 22:14-16)*

I've heard it said that Jesus' sacrifice was predominantly physical, but I wholeheartedly disagree. Anyone who endured crucifixion would endure great physical agony, but to appreciate the fullness of his cup we must take into consideration that his spirit was wounded, as is ours through emotional, mental, and spiritual anguish. But for him, this happened as he bore our sins and was punished in our place. For us, this happens because of the results of our and others' sins. Proverbs 18:14 tells us, "A man's spirit will endure sickness, but a crushed spirit who can bear?" Jesus' spirit was wounded, just as ours is during times of suffering in our lives. So to partake of the cup of Christ involves more than physical anguish, although it usually includes such.

The principal purpose of the Lord's Supper was to remind Christians of Christ's death for sinners, and the death of Christ was the fulfillment of the Passover. Christ was the true sacrifice to which every Passover lamb had been pointing for fifteen hundred years. What the death of the lamb had been to the Israelites in Egypt, his death would be to sinners all over the world. Apart from this, no other reason for his being sacrificed can be found. The Holy Spirit would soon come upon Jesus' followers, substantiate his ministry, and authenticate the full meaning behind the Lord's Supper.

5

SUFFERING AND SALVATION

"I tell you the truth: it is to your advantage that I go away, for if I do not go away, the Helper will not come to you. But if I go, I will send him to you."

JOHN 16:7

Scripture teaches us in Matthew 8:17 that Jesus himself took our infirmities and bore our illnesses on the cross. Matthew was quoting Isaiah 53:4, which also assures us that Christ carried our sorrows. And Luke 4:18 (NKJV) tells us he came to "heal the brokenhearted." We know that all God's words are true. So why do we continue to face trials in our lives? How do we share in the cup of suffering and sorrow *and* walk in the knowledge that Jesus bore our infirmities, sickness, and grief? Why do we still experience pain if Christ Jesus took it upon himself thousands of years ago? If sin was conquered on the cross, why do we battle against it continually? Shouldn't we be totally relieved from sin and suffering once we receive Christ as our Savior?

One part of the answer to these seemingly contradictory statements is best explained by Dallas Anderson, Director of Proclamation Ministries for the Billy Graham Center in Wheaton, Illinois:

> There is an unavoidable sense of frustration and tension that we have to learn to live with while we walk in this life centered around one crucial truth: Not everybody that is prayed for is healed, we will suffer, we will grapple with sin on a daily basis and we will die. It seems contra-

dictive to what we know to be true: Jesus died for our sin, suffering and conquering death.

There are times when we pray and our prayers are answered promptly, miraculously, and without hesitance on God's part, while other times it may seem like our prayers were never heard at all, or at best, the answer is being delayed.

The truth is that Jesus did defeat all of the powers of evil, once and for all on the cross and in his resurrection. By his stripes we are healed. Because he was pierced for our transgressions, we are free. Because he dealt with the chastisement of our sin, we have peace. He conquered death so that we could have life.

Jesus came and preached that "the kingdom of God" had arrived in his coming to earth, and he was equally adamant that the kingdom was coming more fully in the future (John 1:12; Luke 4:18-21; Matthew 19:28). Hence we live in the tension of a "now and not yet" world.

Jesus defeated the power of evil completely, but we still grapple with the onslaught of evil daily. In that, there is an acute awareness that the ultimate victory of God will not see its final completion until Christ comes again. Thus life is lived in the midst of a crooked and perverse generation where sin, suffering, and pain are the norm. We are called to live not as citizens of this evil world, but as citizens of heaven. We are called to accept by faith that we are adopted as God's children by the blood shed by Jesus, but we are also told to work out our salvation with fear and trembling. These seemingly contradictive statements are all true.

In essence, we are caught between two governments. In America when a new president is elected, a team of people is put in place for the purpose of initiating the transfer of power from the old administration to the new. Although the victor is not president until the inauguration, the effect of the election is already at work in the transition. The outgoing president is basically a lame duck no matter what he tries to accomplish because the newly appointed president has the ultimate veto power to override his decisions. Thus the center of focus is on the incoming president and policies, although the old administration appears to be in charge.

This gives us insight to the current situation we find ourselves in today. The church is in effect a transition team. Transition between an administration where there is no room for God, which describes the true sense of the world we inhabit, and one where God is the center of everything, which describes the reality of the coming kingdom. We live in a world where suffering and pain are prominent. However, there are times when the new administration exercises the ultimate veto power over what the old world seeks to bring against us, and intervenes in what we would refer to as a miracle. As we are told in Scripture, we are citizens of the new world while we physically operate in the old.

Jesus has been clearly established as the victor through his work on the cross and in the resurrection. He has won the battle, and the old administration has lost its position as a ruling party. There is coming a day when we shall witness its sealed fate with clarity. The evil one and his cohorts will be cast into the lake of fire. With them will go all traces of the old administration, suffering, evil, pain, and finally, death itself (1 Corinthians 15:26). We have been told by the new administration that during this time of transition we will suffer all the more because of our faith in Jesus, thus leading to our current condition. But this is not the end of the story. Scripture tells us that we will reign with the Son in the new administration. Therefore, we are to focus on the incoming victor and to live in the reality of his new administration even when we still feel the effects of the old. We are not only free to ask for our Father's veto power over the effects of the old but are commanded to ask for it! In doing so, others will see the reality of the new kingdom and join it themselves.

Dallas's understanding of being caught in two worlds, or what he refers to as the "now and not yet" perspective, hits the nail on the head. The world and its inhabitants are in transition, awaiting the Second Coming of the Lord Jesus Christ. When that occurs, death will have no power over life, and all believers will rise in him. We will have no scars, sorrow, disease, or grief. We will live eternally in perfect peace with our Creator, his Son and our Savior, and the Holy Spirit. Oh, how I long for that day and time!

Although we are moving toward a future in eternity, we are caught somewhere in the transition of the present where we still experience pain and suffering in numerous ways—by our own choices, by the poor choices of others, and by the hand of evil—and where we sometimes see miraculous healings of those wounds but at other times do not. We see God deliver people from the pain and anguish of the residual effects of sin, while others wrestle with them their entire life. We sometimes experience the peace that surpasses all understanding, and at other times we have to actively fight against pandemonium.

Keeping the "now and not yet" theory in mind, we must also understand two other crucial elements in relation to suffering—the role of the Holy Spirit and faith.

THE HOLY SPIRIT

Jesus said that he had to depart in order for the Holy Spirit to come (John 16:7). And when the Spirit of God did come, he was given to the church as a promised gift or down payment to confirm to us that Jesus Christ will return (Luke 24:49; John 14:16; Acts 1:5). Believers don't all agree on how or when we receive the Holy Spirit, but the fact remains that he indwells and is accessible to all who have faith.

When we pray and ask the Lord to show us what to do in any specific situation, we are also asking the Holy Spirit to be with us, guide us, and teach us. Scripture tells us that the Spirit of the Lord is evident in a believer's life when:

- the power of sin is no longer in control (Romans 8:2-6),
- self-control is displayed (Galatians 5:22-23),
- prompting or leading is given to the believer (Acts 8:29; Romans 8:14; Galatians 5:16, 25),
  - talents/gifts are manifested in a person's life (1 Corinthians 12:4-11),
  - the strength and power to witness is evident (Acts 1:8; 4:31),
  - the conviction of sin occurs (John 16:8),
  - comfort through difficult times/trials is experienced (John 14:16, 27),
  - we have a teachable heart (1 John 2:27),
  - God's character traits are manifested in the believer's life (Galatians 5:22-23), and
  - inner strength is given (Ephesians 3:16).

Interestingly enough, it was the Holy Spirit who led Jesus into the desert where the Spirit knew he would be tempted by Satan (Matthew 4:1). Does it seem logical that God's Holy Spirit would do the same in our lives? If Christ is our example, then the answer is yes, and for the same reason—so that we may glorify God. Additionally, difficulty in life increases our faith and helps us grow in spiritual maturity, both of which are evidence of the Holy Spirit in our lives. Through the Holy Spirit the believer is controlled by God's desires and is equipped to do all he has called him to do, including the endurance of suffering (Ephesians 5:18-21; Romans 12).

We read in Acts that after Jesus was taken up into heaven, the early Christians were suffering tremendous grief over their loss. But Jesus had promised them a Comforter, and sure enough, at Pentecost they received that comfort through the indwelling of the Holy Spirit. The predominant role of the Holy Spirit is the same now as it was for the early believers—to soothe our grief, fill and control us, and remind us of all of Christ's teachings.

There may be times when we must wait patiently for the fulfillment of a promise. We must cling to what God has told us despite external evidence that may seem to indicate that God has forsaken us. There may be a moment in time when we begin to believe the lie that God doesn't care, has deserted us, or is not invested in our agony, when in fact he has promised the Comforter who will come. There is sometimes a moment of time (that feels like an eternity) between our loss or grief and the fulfillment of a promise. Even Jesus experienced this when he cried out, "My God, my God, why have you forsaken me?"

The apostle Paul tells us in Acts 20 that the Holy Spirit warned him that he would face prison and other hardships. His response? "I do not account my life of any value nor as precious to myself, if only I may finish my course and the ministry that I received from the Lord Jesus" (v. 24). The "ministry" he spoke of was that of testifying to the gospel of God's grace, which as we saw in the previous chapter is always sufficient when needed.

Further, during Paul's hardships he said:

We put no obstacle in anyone's way, so that no fault may be found with our ministry, but as servants of God we commend ourselves in every way: by great endurance, in afflictions, hardships, calamities, beatings, imprisonments, riots, labors, sleepless nights, hunger; by purity, knowledge, patience, kindness, the Holy Spirit, genuine love; by truthful speech, and the power of God; with the weapons of righteousness for the right hand and for the left; through honor and dishonor, through slander and praise. We are treated as impostors, and yet are true; as unknown, and yet well known; as dying, and behold, we live; as punished, and yet not killed; as sorrowful, yet always rejoicing; as poor, yet making many rich; as having nothing, yet possessing everything. (2 Corinthians 6:3-10)

When you lean on the Spirit, he will teach you the difference between truth and falsehood, and that in itself will promote healing. He will convict you of sin, which will, through the steps of repentance, provide restoration to your soul. He will guide and lead you in the right direction. He will prompt you to do good and not evil, and he will meet you in the midst of your suffering, minister to you, and guide you into healing for your specific situation. But accessing the power of the Holy Spirit requires faith.

FAITH'S POWER

In the thought-provoking film *Simon Birch*, the main character is a small boy born with a weak heart who is not expected to survive infancy. But Simon surprises everyone and not only lives beyond babyhood but for another twelve years. Throughout his life Simon firmly believes that God spared his life for a reason, a purpose only he can fulfill. As his life unfolds, Simon searches for that destiny until he finally discovers it.

But all odds are against Simon. Not only is he small in stature and physically deformed, his parents have no use for him, and he is scorned by society. Throughout the movie Simon is taunted and teased both by his peers and by adults. Everyone from his pastor to his best friend warns him to stop believing this divine fantasy. But Simon remains convinced. He can't explain why he knows God has a plan for his life, and he has no proof for it, but he knows it's true. He's convinced he's an instrument of God and that God will somehow use him to carry out his plan.

Eventually Simon's faith and reality come face-to-face. Every character in the movie, as well as every audience member, realizes that Simon did have a God-given purpose and that he fulfilled it in a way that only he could.

At one point in the movie Simon says, "I don't need proof [of God's plan]. I have faith." Faith, my friend, is not something we attain, but something we already possess—something with which we were born. Scripture does not tell us to find or create our faith but rather to *build* our faith (Luke 17:5). We build on something we already possess. Like most living things, faith is either nurtured and grows or it is neglected and dies. How unfortunate that circumstances can sometimes tear down our childlike faith before it has the opportunity to flourish.

Such was the case in my life. My own childhood was horrendous. It was filled with an array of abuse and abandonment, but somehow, deep inside, I believed God had a plan for me. I didn't know what that plan was or how I'd accomplish it, but I knew that God existed and that there was a purpose to my life. Sometimes I lost that hope, and when I did I wandered aimlessly through life, seeking refuge from a variety of unhealthy sources. Every decision I made at that time brought me misery and led me into further bondage and suffering.

Even as a believer there have been times when I have not had faith in Christ. For long periods I have become devastated by my circumstances. I misplaced my focus and remained in the wilderness until once again I saw clearly the goal that Christ had for me. But that required that I trust what God had promised in his Word and believe in him even though I'd been let down again and again by others. That took faith.

Mere faith, not faith in Christ but just faith, allows children to blindly believe in Santa Claus and the Easter Bunny. Faith is why we believe in princes and fairy godmothers. Faith is why we believe that Jesus loves us, died for us, and will never forsake us as we grapple with our heartache, pain, and agony. But as we grow and mature, we learn that there is no Santa, no Easter Bunny, and no fairy godmother, and we even begin to challenge Jesus' existence—is he someone who loves us unconditionally, or is he too a fictional character?

Genuine faith is knowing, believing, and standing on the truth even when circumstances or feelings suggest otherwise. Knowing is different than wondering. *The foundation of our journey must be knowing.* We know because the Bible tells us, and God confirms the truth through the Holy Spirit. If the Bible says it, then we must believe in faith that it's true. And if it's true, then we can stand on it, regardless of the circumstances. When used as designed, the Bible will bring healing, hope, encouragement, and trust as the Holy Spirit, in response to our faith, ministers, teaches us, and leads us. Obviously, the Holy Spirit does not confirm the existence of Santa Claus or fairy godmothers, for God cannot lie and will never mislead us.

If we do not believe the Bible to be true, then we cannot be born again and therefore do not receive healing, hope, and encouragement from the Holy Spirit. Accepting Jesus as our Savior is predicated on knowing that God's Word is true, knowing that Jesus died for us, knowing that he has forgiven us, and knowing that he has a plan for us. But if we do not believe, it is because we do not trust that what God has said is true. Belief + Trust = Faith.

We must have faith like Simon Birch, believing that God has a plan for our lives, a plan that only we can fulfill with his help. And the plan is available in a detailed, written, profound, and yet understandable blueprint called the Bible, and it is confirmed through the Holy Spirit. If we believe what the Bible says, trust what it says, and stand in faith on what it says, then *all things are possible* for us as we walk in the will of God. Faith is an action, and it requires us to step out into the unknown and believe and trust in something, despite what our flesh and the world might say.

Faith can heal, motivate, and cleanse us. It moves mountains, provides our every need, and most importantly gives us eternal life. Faith reminds me of a two-year-old child standing on a porch while his father encourages him to jump. As the father steps back, he opens his arms wide and says to the child, "Jump! I'll catch you, I promise! Jump!" Some children react immediately because they trust their father will catch them. They bend at the knees, extend their arms, and with every fiber of their growing body spring off the porch into their father's arms. Nothing hinders such a child's trust in his father. We need to build the same kind of faith in our heavenly Father. If God said it, we know we can depend upon it.

But we know that some children hesitate. Their father hasn't always been there to catch them when they fell, let alone when they jumped. Or their father plays games with them that might lead to mistrust. Sometimes he catches them; sometimes he doesn't. And when he doesn't, he might say that bumps and bruises, cuts and scars make a person stronger, more self-reliant, and children shouldn't depend on anyone but themselves. In truth, such unkind actions and words encourage doubt, insecurity, and a severe lack of trust in an earthly father. In contrast, our heavenly Father is always there to catch us when we trust him and believe he is there. With arms open wide, he promises, "I am here waiting for you. It is safe to jump into my arms. I will not let you fall, I promise. I give you my word."

In the fall of 1998 I had the pleasure of meeting and developing a friendship with Joni Eareckson Tada. At that time Joni had been in a wheelchair for over thirty-one years. She became a quadriplegic in 1967 from a diving accident. I was a prison chaplain, and Joni and her staff worked with our people to form a program to restore wheelchairs for those who were physically disabled.

During a conversation over lunch, Joni and I discussed other types of disabilities that cause suffering apart from physical ones—emotional, mental, and even spiritual. Some of us are spiritually disabled because we were born into homes that worshiped false gods or no god, or homes that knew the Law but forgot grace. Other times it's an emotional disability due to abuse by a parent, guardian, or spouse or a result of choices we have made. Many people are mentally disabled due to verbal abuse, genetics, mental illness, satanic ritual abuse, and more. All disabilities cause suffering to some extent.

A disability is anything that incapacitates a person in part or whole, thereby preventing or limiting "normal" day-to-day activities and inevitably causing suffering to some extent. In my counseling ministry I have met hundreds of people who cannot function in society because of a specific disability. They are just as disabled as a person who is bound to a wheelchair, but in a different way. In their day-to-day struggles they have lost focus on the fact that God has a plan for their lives.

Some of the most gifted and talented people I have met are behind bars. Many of them suffered through childhoods that few of us could have survived without ending up in prison ourselves—or dead. We all have a past with its own wounds and failures, and everyone's past influences his or her well-being, decisions, and current circumstances—emotionally, mentally, physically, and especially spiritually.

But my ministry has also allowed me to meet thousands of people who are not behind bars, yet still live in a prison. Some have chosen this path, while others had it forced upon them by the choices of others or a combination of both. But because they have lost focus on God, they feel hopeless and unable to be used by him. Without vision, men perish. When there is no vision, there is no hope and in turn no goal—nothing at which to aim. What good is an arrow without a target? Our vision as believers must be God's vision for our lives—achieving that which is imperishable through Jesus Christ. This is not to say that God is opposed to giving us the desires of our hearts. However, our desires must be aligned with God's desires, which are always consistent with the written Word of God (see Psalm 37:3-4; 2 Timothy 3:14-17). Everything contrary to fulfilling God's will for our lives will fail and will ultimately lead to eternal destitution.

Following her diving accident, Joni initially felt hopeless. Filled with anger toward God, she was consumed by a "why me?" attitude. But this led her nowhere. Confined to her bed, she became suicidal and ineffective for Christ. She lost her vision. Eventually she submitted to God's plan for her life, and in the years since then he has used her disability for his glory, helping literally thousands of people. Joni has been more successful in Christ without the use of her legs than most who have total use of their bodies. She has fulfilled part of his plan for her life, though God's not finished with her yet! No one else could have accomplished what Joni has. Not because she's so amazing, but because God is, and he set Joni apart to fulfill that purpose. In turn, she made herself a willing vessel, disability and all. She didn't understand this at the time of the accident, but she eventually came to believe that God's promises are not lies but truth. She trusted what his Word said. Belief + Trust = Faith.

Amazing, isn't it, that while bound to a wheelchair she can stand on the truth, apply it to her life, and change the lives of people around her. This is faith in action, and it is the trumpet call for the Holy Spirit to engage his power. God will do no less for any of us who willingly bring our disabilities and suffering and wounds to the foot of the cross and allow him to use them. He can and will use our disabilities to honor him. There is nothing we have experienced that he can't use (see Romans 8:28).

So what's stopping us? We place ordinary, worldly limits on an extraordinary, heavenly God. He has no equal, and yet we compare him to our own limitations. There is nothing he cannot do, yet we underestimate him. We are foolish people who have the potential for incredible power through Christ, but this power lies dormant due to our lack of trust, our fear of the future, our lack of knowledge of who we are, and our refusal to use a resource that is in almost every person's home—the infallible Word of God.

Once again, if we do not have hope, it's because we have no spiritual vision, and without vision, we spiritually perish. Our vision must be God's vision, and his vision for us is described in his Word. So we must learn his Word, stand on it, and apply it to our lives. That will result in a healing unlike anything we've ever experienced in our lives before.

Moreover, many of us have been disabled by the enemy of our souls. The power to heal from that injury is found in God's Word. Will you begin to use its magnificent power? Or will you remain disabled, hopeless, and ineffective?

"Faith is the assurance of things hoped for, the conviction of things not seen" (Hebrews 11:1). "Things hoped for" and "not seen" are visions for the future. The fact is, the invisible is more tangible and permanent than the visible. Faith is the foundation of all things in Christ, including transformation. We shouldn't let life's circumstances shipwreck our faith. We can trust, we can believe, and we can walk in faith. We should ask the Lord to increase our faith, remembering that faith comes by hearing and hearing by the Word of God (Romans 10:17).

We must understand and acknowledge, if we are honest, that we attain an intimacy and dependency upon Christ when we suffer that we probably would not seek apart from it. He wants us to taste the fruit of vulnerability and surety through intimacy with him and to be so satisfied that we will never be inclined to settle for imitations. He knows that when we are in excruciating pain, our conversations with him have more depth and are more authentic than the ones we offer halfheartedly when life is going well. It is in the darkest nights that we exercise faith and believe that God is present and able. It is when death lingers at our door that we honestly begin to examine our motives, repent, and seek his grace through the Holy Spirit. It is when we've been stripped of our identity or leveled by loss or when death threatens to steal a loved one that we finally cry out to God with passion and in humility. It is when our fears have become reality, when we've loved and lost, when we are stripped of all of our health, when the reality of life being a vapor comes face-to-face with our humanity that we finally seek the Lord's greatness and see ourselves for who we really are—feeble and weak, fragile and vulnerable, meek and lowly humans in need of a Savior, a Hero, an Abba, a Father, a Friend, and a Comforter. Humility feels a lot like being small and weak, but when we are small he is great, and when we are weak he is strong.

6

Sorrow to the Point of Death

Then Jesus went with them to a place called Gethsemane, and he said to his disciples, "Sit here, while I go over there and pray." And taking with him Peter and the two sons of Zebedee, he began to be sorrowful and troubled.

MATTHEW 26:36-37

I had everything I needed to complete the job successfully. I had gone to the store early that morning and purchased two boxes of the strongest over-the-counter sleeping pills I could find—forty-eight extra-strength to be exact. I had gone to bed the night before believing full well that the next day would be the last day I'd spend on earth. I had thought heavily about what I would say in the note I would leave for my mother and my two children—Charlene, who was three, and Paul, who was two. When I awoke the next morning, I sat on the edge of my bed and wept as I put what I'd rehearsed in my heart the night before on paper. Later I filled the largest glass I could find to the rim with liquid to wash the pills down. I was an unbeliever, and I had no hope.

As I leaned back into the pillows on my bed, one by one I swallowed the pills that promised to end the shame, self-hatred, unforgiveness, and bitterness toward the men who had wasted my childhood on their selfish desires. The pills would put a permanent end to the haunting memories and the violation of my innocence that relentlessly taunted me day and night. Even then, at twenty years of age, I could hear their voices and feel their touches as if it all had just happened. They had been persistent enemies to my fragile femininity from as early as I could remember, and as I grew into a teenager the memories religiously fed my downward spiral of drugs, alcohol, and promiscuity. When the cocaine, booze, and multiple failed attempts at love didn't make their voices and touches cease, I felt I had only one way to escape the relentless violations to my soul and the shame that flooded my being—ending my life. After the last pill was taken, I lay flat on my bed, anxiously waiting for my assailants' voices to be silenced and for their touches to end.

By God's divine intervention, a miracle to say the least, I did not die, obviously. That had not been my first attempt, but it would be my last, almost taking me into a chasm of death. I could feel my spirit leaving my body but also a peace I had never experienced before permeating every part of my being. Just when I thought my life was over, I was graciously given another chance. The truth was, I didn't really *want* to die—I just didn't know how to live.

"Overwhelmed with sorrow to the point of death" is how Scripture describes the soul of Jesus in the Garden of Gethsemane (Matthew 26:38, NIV). The soul is the heart, mind, will, and life of a person. While Jesus was facing death as a sacrifice for our sins and not as an option to the pain he was grappling with on earth, his example does lead us to talk intimately about the depth to which sorrow can descend. His imminent death was in no way the same as the impending death of someone who has chosen to end his or her life, but he does understand the intense fear that we experience when we are near death. Of course, those who are dying from a terminal illness or are near death for some other reason can also benefit from the discussion in this chapter, but I want to focus particularly on those who are contemplating suicide.

Suicide takes the lives of over twenty-five thousand people in the United States a year.[1] Over a million try annually, with many being hospitalized.[2] Suicide is the tenth highest killer in the United States. More people die from suicide than from homicide.[3] This is obviously not something we should avoid discussing, especially when we realize that taking one's life is often done after victims of suicide have experienced a loss (relational, social, work-related, or financial) of someone or something significant in their lives.[4]

When we come to the brutal state of mind where death is not only seen as an option but as our only hope for relief from pain, we are utterly shattered on the ground level of a mental and emotional hell. We cannot go any farther down into the depths of despair. We've hit rock bottom, are at the lowest point imaginable, and find ourselves in a place that literally takes our breath away. Thousands of people find themselves at this point after a tragedy, and many never make it back from that crucial point of life and death as I so miraculously did. But it doesn't have to be that way. Jesus too took the journey to the end of life (though not in suicide). He confronted death, so we could choose life. Isn't it ironic and amazing—he died so we could live. We too must confront death in its most brutal form and must choose life through the Lord. In order to do so, we must look honestly at the option to live or die that awaits our choice once we hit rock bottom. First, let's look at suicide through God's eyes.

GOD'S PERSPECTIVE

I've sat in many therapy groups as a counselor and have heard countless people refer to hitting rock bottom. Their description of such a place is generally negative. It's an undesirable place to be because they've lost anything and everything of value to them, and their devastation left them on the brink of taking their own life. When considering the phrase *rock bottom* from God's view, however, we must get to its root to understand what it really means. *Webster's New World Dictionary* defines a rock as "anything like or suggesting a rock, as in strength or stability; a firm support, basis, or refuge." The word *bottom* is defined as "the lowest or last place or position. The part on which something rests; the base."

If we take these definitions literally, *rock bottom* means "to rest on a strong, stable, supportive base, where we are sheltered and protected." Scripture often refers to Jesus as the rock in our lives. First Corinthians 10:3-4 states, "All ate the same spiritual food, and all drank the same spiritual drink. For they drank from the spiritual Rock that followed them, and the Rock was Christ."

If we use Webster's definition in this verse, what is being said is that Christ is our strength, our firm support, our stability and refuge. Jesus' parable in Matthew 7 is about a man who built his house on the foundation of a rock and another who built his house upon sand. Verses 24-27 state:

> *"Everyone then who hears these words of mine and does them will be like a wise man who built his house on the rock. And the rain fell, and the floods came, and the winds blew and beat on that house, but it did not fall, because it had been founded on the rock. And everyone who hears these words of mine and does not do them will be like a foolish man who built his house on the sand. And the rain fell, and the floods came, and the winds blew and beat against that house, and it fell, and great was the fall of it."*

In this parable Christ is again the rock, the foundation (bottom), our stability, our security, our support, and our strength. The house refers to our lives and our walk with Christ. The rain, the rising streams, and the winds are the trials and temptations that come against us. What are we building our lives on—the sand or the Rock?

This question leads me to the definition of the word *bottom*. *Bottom* is seen in two ways. First, it is the lowest or last place or position. We all, as humans, have a natural desire to be first. We are programmed by the world that being last, being at the bottom, means failure. This is a distortion of the truth. We are told in Philippians 2:5-7 that we should follow Christ's example:

> *Have this mind among yourselves, which is yours in Christ Jesus, who, though he was in the form of God, did not count equality with God a thing to be grasped, but made himself nothing, taking the form of a servant, being born in the likeness of men.*

Jesus himself said, "The greatest among you shall be your servant. Whoever exalts himself will be humbled, and whoever humbles himself will be exalted" (Matthew 23:11). Oh, how hard it is to die to self, to be a servant, to not exalt ourselves!

Second, *bottom* is referred to as the part on which something rests. Resting isn't easy, particularly if you're like me and wrestle with the whys and what ifs of everything that occurs. Because most of my youth was out of my control (especially all the physical and sexual abuse), I was determined as a teenager and adult always to keep control of myself and my circumstances. Resting (not to mention depending) on the Lord, allowing him to have control of my life, has been difficult. But Psalm 37:7 tells us to "rest in the LORD, and wait patiently for Him" (NKJV).

Waiting and resting go hand in hand. One of my favorite verses is Isaiah 40:31: "they who wait for the LORD shall renew their strength; they shall mount up with wings like eagles; they shall run and not be weary; they shall walk and not faint."

Looking at the times in my life when I've hit rock bottom and made the choice to rest in the arms of the Rock, I can see that those were times of great restoration and healing. However, from a human perspective hitting rock bottom is a matter of grave hopelessness.

THE HUMAN PERSPECTIVE

In the midst of grief, death can sometimes be appealing, if not inviting. Chronic pain caused by the loss of a loved one, a mental illness, or a sudden depletion of health or finances among other circumstances can, without spiritual intervention, lead to thoughts of taking one's own life. While persons considering such an option may have received Christ as their Savior and have at times tried to build their foundation on the Rock, their faith presently resides on shifting sand.

When we come to the place where we are contemplating suicide, we have rejected faith in Christ and are doubting that what he says in his Word is true. And because we have rejected that faith, we are temporarily incapable of seeing things through a spiritual lens and instead are viewing them from a human perspective. As a result, we have lost hope, and as Scripture tells us, "Hope deferred makes the heart sick" (Proverbs 13:12).

Once we have lost hope, we lose our desire to live. Often this hope is deferred and the vision lost because we have, in our human fragility, enmeshed ourselves too thoroughly with what we have lost. In other words, our identity has become so interwoven with something that we are stripped of our identity and lose all hope for life when it's taken away. Behind the preceding statement is the fact that God has vowed to strip us of anything that we have placed above him. While that is not always the case when we experience a loss, we must consider the possibility that we have made that which we are grieving more important to ourselves than he is.

There are seven biblical examples of suicide, all of which reveal a loss of hope and vision:

• Abimelech (Judges 9): A warrior-king of Israel, Abimelech lacked any kind of affirmation or certainty in his personal identity. While Abimelech attempted to exterminate a large number of unarmed civilians as he had previously done, a woman dropped a millstone on his head. His disrespect for women was so great that he promptly asked his armor-bearer to kill him with his sword so people could not say he'd been killed by a woman (vv. 52-54).

• Samson (Judges 13–16): After he was captured and blinded, Samson was chained between two pillars at the Philistine temple. After asking God for strength, he pushed the pillars apart, knowing that would cause the collapse of the building. As a result, he died along with the thousands of people inside (16:25-30).

• Saul (1 Samuel 9–31): During a war against the Philistines, Saul's three sons—Jonathan, Abinadab, and Malchi-shua—were killed, and he himself was seriously wounded. He was overcome with stress and grief and felt rejected and like a failure. As a result, he asked his armor-bearer to kill him. When the armor-bearer refused, Saul took a sword and "fell upon it" (31:4).

• Saul's armor-bearer: Impulsive and scared, Saul's armor-bearer fell on his own sword, causing his own death (1 Samuel 31:5).

• Ahithophel (2 Samuel 17): In his attempt to come up with a plan to kill King David, Ahithophel became bitter when his advice was not followed. Scripture tells us he "set his house in order and hanged himself, and he died" (v. 23).

• Zimri (1 Kings 16:15-20): A rebel, Zimri had a problem with authority. When his city was besieged and taken, he became distressed over the sins he had committed, and "went into the citadel of the king's house and burned the king's house over him with fire and died" (v. 18).

• Judas: Judas betrayed Jesus for thirty pieces of silver and then was rejected by the high priests and elders. He was depressed and consumed with greed and guilt. As a result, he hanged himself (Matthew 27:3-5).

For the men mentioned above, suicide became a permanent solution to some temporary problems. Samson was trying to rectify his past mistakes, three of the men were wounded and didn't want to linger in sickness, and Ahithophel feared death would consume him once King David got ahold of him anyway. Saul, Ahithophel, and Zimri felt rejected either by God, man, or both, and Judas was under the control of Satan. Regardless of why they committed suicide, the core belief was the same: *life is not worth living.* All of these men had become spiritually sick at the time of their deaths. They had lost their hope and vision.

Each one of these examples could have been rectified through dependence upon Christ and the Word of God. The Bible tells us that God created us in his image and that he has great plans for our lives (Genesis 1:26-27; Jeremiah 29:11). But the people considered above gave up on those truths, instead buying into the lie that they had nothing more to live for than that which they had already accomplished. The plans God had for them came to an abrupt end when they chose to take their lives into their own hands.

One of the most crucial lessons that Jesus taught believers while he was on earth was that death and destruction are the work of "the thief" who comes only to "steal and kill and destroy" (John 10:10). We are told that the Devil is "a murderer" and "the father of lies" (John 8:44). When we are faced with thoughts of suicide, we must realize where that thought is originating from—the one who wants to steal our lives and kill and destroy us—Satan. Thus we must take every thought captive to the obedience of Jesus Christ (2 Corinthians 10:4-6). Satan does not want you to live because he knows your death at your own hand will cause further wounds, more hopelessness, and potentially more death (spiritually and physically). Further, the Devil does not want you to carry out the plan that God has for you because then he is conquered by Christ who strengthens you.

Jesus came so that we could have life and experience it to the full (John 10:10). Life belongs to him. If you've given Jesus reign in your heart, your body is the "temple," the home, the residence of the Holy Spirit (1 Corinthians 6:19-20). You are not your own to do whatever your emotions prompt you to do. You have been bought with a price and are commanded to honor God with your body—which means life, not death.

Earlier in this chapter I shared with you that during my last suicide attempt I didn't really want to die—I just didn't know how to live. Let me share with you how to regain the passion to live again.

Regaining the Passion to Live

The first step toward life is choosing to stand on the truth even though you are wavering. Second Corinthians 10:5-6 says, "We destroy arguments and every lofty opinion raised against the knowledge of God, and take every thought captive to obey Christ."

"The knowledge of God" that you have has to do with who you are in Christ, his Word, and the plans he has for your life. In the context of our topic, "arguments" are disagreements and disputes within you that provide a course of reasoning offering seemingly logical reasons for you to take your own life. An example may be that you have nothing more to live for now that your loved one is gone. That belief implies that your loved one was the reason you lived. As a believer, that is not true—Jesus is the reason you live. You must break the bondage of the lie to live in freedom and truth.

A "lofty opinion" (NIV, "pretension") is a claim to something, such as a privilege or right. If your life is your own, you have the "right" to do whatever you desire with it, we are told. However, as a believer your life belongs to Jesus Christ. You were bought at a price, and thus you belong to him who paid that cost (1 Corinthians 6:19-20).

How can we take these "arguments" and "lofty opinions" that have set themselves up against "the knowledge of God" captive to Jesus Christ? By speaking them out to him through prayer and asking him to give us strength and hope for that very moment in time. Sometimes we must do this process a hundred times a day. We must do whatever we have to do to survive today, trusting and believing that God will follow through with his Word to "reward those who seek him" (Hebrews 11:6). In doing so, our hope will increase, and hopelessness will decrease. Psalm 33:20-22 tells us:

Our soul waits for the LORD;
he is our help and our shield.
For our heart is glad in him,
because we trust in his holy name.
Let your steadfast love, O LORD, be upon us,
even as we hope in you.

As we wait in hope for the Lord, he promises to give us rest from our problems: "Come to me, all you who labor are heavy laden, and I will give you rest" (Matthew 11:28).

The next thing I encourage you to do is to be honest and talk with someone else about your thoughts about ending your life. Hiding or stuffing your feelings and thoughts will only breed like-minded ones that will lead you into further despair. Call a trusted pastor, another believer, a friend, or someone you feel comfortable sharing with and talk about what's going on. Be brutally honest. Sometimes a counselor is needed. Whatever you do, when you have thoughts of killing yourself, do not wait to talk openly with someone. Recognize the urgency of seeing and talking to someone *now*. If you have no one to talk to, you can call the Focus on the Family hotline at 800-232-6459 during normal business hours. Their Christian therapists can help you find a godly counselor in your area, provide immediate crisis intervention, and provide solid, biblical counseling. Call 9-1-1 if you have a plan and intend on carrying it out.

While it may seem that this is going overboard, I assure you it is not. Your life is important, and you may need immediate help to preserve it. Sometimes the assaults of the enemy of our souls are so intense that we need others to intercede for us spiritually and physically. You must realize that Satan doesn't want you to talk to someone, because he knows if you are alone, you are weak. Break through your silence and tell someone *now*.

Jesus' Sorrow to the Point of Death

Matthew 26 tells us that Jesus began to be "sorrowful and troubled" in Gethsemane (v. 37). The Greek words used in this passage in the original manuscripts mean "to cause sorrow or grief" or "to be sad." In the Gospel of Mark, the author uses stronger, more adamant language, saying Jesus was "deeply distressed" (14:33, NIV, NKJV), meaning he was alarmed. None of the language used by either writer refers to a flippant emotional state that could be easily eased in a moment's time by a good joke or an exquisite bouquet of flowers. Instead, they describe a deep wounding of the heart, a never-ending pain that reaches to the marrow of one's soul, acute anguish.

Jesus was suffering for us—for our sins, our sorrows, our restoration, our healing. He was also agonizing over the expected separation that would tear him away from his Father for the first and last time in all eternity. Imagine that for a moment. Consider how you feel when you are separated from God because of your sin. Take into account the depth of pain experienced from every illness you've ever experienced, may be experiencing, or will experience. Ponder the chaos that you grapple with and the peace you so adamantly longed for before you knew Jesus Christ as your Savior, and even now perhaps in the midst of suffering. Contemplate that grieving of the Holy Spirit within you—the loneliness, the emptiness, the shame, the conviction, the desperate need to be restored. Now multiply that by every person who has ever existed. As much as we try, we cannot fathom the physical pain, the emotional agony or grief, or the mental anguish Jesus endured on our behalf, let alone the spiritual agony of being forsaken by the Father as Jesus took our sins upon himself.

Scripture tells us that Jesus confessed to Peter and the sons of Zebedee that his soul was "overwhelmed with sorrow to the point of death" (Matthew 26:38, NIV). Nothing in that statement gives the interpreter the impression that Jesus was struggling with something minor. It was a life-or-death situation, and his words imply that the pain was so excruciating that he could die simply by experiencing it. Many of us can relate to that pain, though of course not fully because we are not Jesus and we are not bearing the sins of the whole world.

Believers are told that we will not experience more than we can handle, and while that is true, it often seems as though we are pushed to the very end of the proverbial envelope of anguish as we waver between life and death. We feel we are at the breaking point. And yet when we call upon God, he intervenes with supernatural strength, and we are able to keep going. Such was the case with Jesus. Scripture tells us, "there appeared to him an angel from heaven, strengthening him" (Luke 22:43). But even after that empowering, heavenly intervention, our Savior continued in anguish. Despite his praying, "his sweat became like great drops of blood falling down to the ground" (v. 44).

For thousands of years critics have debated whether or not Jesus actually bled out of the pores of his body, an actual physiological phenomenon called hematohidrosis, or whether the sweating was so profuse that it just *looked* like blood dripping from a wound. But by focusing on that debate, the reader bypasses a critical point—the severity of his agony. It would be equally absurd for us to get into a debate that critically analyzes the physical extremity and manifestation of our anguish. That would minimize or dismiss our experience entirely.

Luke, a physician, is the only Gospel writer to mention the bloody sweat that poured from Jesus' flesh. Whether this was due to the intense spiritual agony Jesus was experiencing or the anticipation of it, one thing is clear—our Savior was under excessive pressure, pain, and stress. It was not the impending physical anguish that caused such an outpouring from his flesh, but the spiritual, emotional, and mental agony that hovered over him and threatened to consume him in the Garden and in the hours to follow.

Jesus had already asked his Father once to take the cup away from him, then submitted to his Father's will not to take it away. Instead God sent an angel to minister to his Son, to strengthen him in this dark hour. Scripture tells us that as a result Jesus prayed more earnestly, so much so that "his sweat became like great drops of blood falling down to the ground." The point of this passage is that while God does not always deliver us instantly, that does not mean he won't give us the supernatural strength to endure the trial. Further, we must understand that even though we are faithful and pray earnestly, we may very well endure even more assaults from the hand of the enemy and even more difficult circumstances.

In the Garden of Gethsemane Satan had his hour of power and darkness when it *seemed* that he reigned mightily over the Son of God. But he did not, and he knew he did not. It was an illusion, a black-magic trick by our enemy, a delusion, trickery, and deception. God the Father was in control, even in Jesus' darkest hour. Equally so, in our own lives the enemy of our souls has what appears to be his moment in time when he holds the bitter cup of suffering up to our lips and hovers over us with a spirit of gloom, licking his lips in anticipation of our fall away from God and into his wretched arms. We can pray, as Jesus did, to be relieved of drinking the cup of suffering, as Moses pled with God to allow him to not die but rather to enter the Promised Land, as Paul did about the thorn in the flesh, as David did for his ill-fated child, and as Hezekiah did to live. But at some point we must come to the place where Jesus did—submission to the will of God.

"Not as I will, but as you will," Jesus told the Father. Knowing how much he wanted relief, I can imagine how hard it must have been to muster up the strength to say those eight words. But he did it—for the Father's glory and for our salvation.

7

SLEEPING THROUGH
THE PAIN

*When he rose from prayer and went back to the disciples, he found them
asleep, exhausted from sorrow.*

LUKE 22:45, NIV

"Exhausted from sorrow," the disciples slept through a time when
Jesus needed them the most. He had warned them, saying, "Pray
that you will not fall into temptation" (Luke 22:40, NIV), then withdrew
from them to pray by himself. Jesus did not ask the disciples to pray for
him because of the looming destruction of his body or because he
needed strength to endure. His request was for them to pray that *they*
would not fall into temptation.

The Gospels of Matthew and Mark reveal that Jesus went away
and returned three times to find the men sleeping. In response he said,
"The spirit indeed is willing, but the flesh is weak" (Matthew 26:41).
The Bible passages stating that the disciples were "exhausted from sorrow" and Jesus' comment that their spirit was willing but their bodies
weak give the impression that the disciples may have been grappling
with anticipatory grief regarding his pending death. What form of
temptation did he want them to resist through prayer? He feared they
would fall into unbelief, where hopelessness is found and vision is
lost.

The disciples were indeed grappling with the effects of anticipatory
grief, and without intimacy with God, without receiving his strength
through prayer, they would not be strong enough not to fall.

LIFE THROUGH THE EYES OF A DISCIPLE

The men had been having a good day—that is, until the Lord's Supper. Passover had been a joyous occasion, celebrating the release of the Israelites from Egypt through the mighty power of God, a time of celebration. But the mood changed entirely when, seemingly out of nowhere, Jesus implemented the Lord's Supper and began talking about his imminent betrayal during dinner.

All twelve disciples partook of the bread that symbolized Jesus' broken body and the cup that pictured the new covenant in his blood that would be poured out for them. Then Jesus dropped a proverbial bomb by saying, "But the hand of him who is going to betray me is with mine on the table. The Son of Man will go as it has been decreed, but woe to that man who betrays him" (Luke 22:21-22, NIV).

The unification among the men suddenly gave way to both internal and external conflict, creating separation among them as they each began to speculate which of them might do such a terrible thing. Then we are told that they began to argue among themselves about who was the greatest (Luke 22:24). Jesus exposed Judas' heart, cursing the day he was born, and humbled them all by giving them the biblical standard for greatness. His words were so penetrating and convicting that a great sadness came upon them (Matthew 26:22). After they finished supper, Jesus dropped what seemed to be the final blow to their egos and future: "You will all fall away, for it is written, 'I will strike the shepherd, and the sheep will be scattered'" (Mark 14:27).

Everything Jesus had ever said up to that point had been true and had occurred as he had stated. So there was no reason for them to doubt what he was saying. Suddenly what he had been telling them for the past three years was upon them: he was leaving, and they would all betray him. He would be crucified. They would all forsake him; they would all scatter. His ministry would end.

I can only imagine that they were scrambling to put meaning behind all the fractured sentences they could conjure up that he'd said over the last three years. In all of their humanity and in an unconscious desire to feed their sinful nature, I can hear them asking the question that runs thick through my own veins: *What about me?*

That's the question we all are faced with in the midst of tragedy. "What's going to happen to me now that my mate has died?" "Who am I now that I've lost my job?" "Who will I become now that I'm divorced?" "Who am I now that I've been stripped of my finances?" "What does my future look like without my child in my life?"

No doubt many troubling questions ran through the minds of the disciples. As far as they could see, their ministry was over. They'd given up various careers to follow Jesus, and now that he was about to die, where would that leave them? Who would they be after Jesus was gone? Where would they go? What would they do? He had been their comfort, support, encouragement, and security as they ventured into their ministries. They had invested their most sacred and intimate selves with him, sharing all their possessions, hopes, and dreams. Suddenly their investment became not only threatened but potentially shattered. The potential death of their Lord would probably disrupt their lives irreparably.

These men were not guilty of selfishness, for it is natural to wonder where we will go and how we will live after a tragedy. Instead, they were guilty of living in the moment instead of by the promise. And in doing so they grappled with grief, slept, lost their vision, became hopeless, and eventually fell into temptation and betrayed their Lord. We can easily fall into the same errors.

Grappling with Grief

When we consider the emotional and mental distress of the disciples leading up to Jesus' final days on earth and the anticipatory grief they experienced in the Garden, it is not surprising that they were found sleeping during such a crucial moment in time.

There is no doubt that the words Jesus spoke over dinner haunted these men as they left the Passover meal and journeyed to the Garden. Jesus had unequivocally told them that they would all forsake him, to their shame. To add fuel to the fire, Jesus had told them he would be crucified, a horrific, violent way to watch someone you love die. The anticipation of such a death is enough to spur severe shock, anxiety, and distress.

Anyone who has lost a loved one can recall the harsh words

announcing the death or the expectation that life would soon end. No matter how such news comes, it hits like an avalanche, resulting in heartache, shock, and disbelief. Few blows to the human spirit are as great as this. At no other time in life are we so acutely aware of having to put one foot in front of the other in order to get through the day. Life moves in extremely painful slow motion and feels like a horrifying nightmare from which we cannot awake.

Grief is often emotionally intense and includes feelings such as sorrow, anguish, anger, regret, longing, fear, and deprivation. Physically it produces exhaustion, emptiness, tension, sleeplessness, or loss of appetite. If we fail to express our grief at the time of loss, the pain can remain constant as we invest so much energy in suppressing our feelings. In order to initiate the healing process we must allow ourselves to share our grief and to release our pain, fears, and heartache to God—something the disciples were asked to do by Jesus but didn't allow themselves to do during those moments in the Garden. Instead they fell into grief and let it wash over them, immobilizing them for the moment of testing yet to come.

Had the disciples gone to prayer as the Lord Jesus suggested and expressed their fear and pain to their Father in heaven, their anguish would not have been continual but instead would have only periodically washed over them as they worked through the grief process.

One of the most important aspects of dealing with loss is to realize that the process of grief is a natural, innate, God-given means to accept and by which to live in spite of the circumstances. An especially harmful belief held by some Christians is that God doesn't want us to grieve. As Ella Wheeler Wilcox said in her famous poem "Solitude," "Laugh, and the world laughs with you; weep, and you weep alone." We are led to believe that it's morbid or even offensive to talk about death. A public display of emotions is not considered appropriate in our society, sometimes even in Christian society, nor is a loss of composure. Although few people say it directly, many tend to think that we are to simply let go and move on quickly. This is contrary to our God-given need to express our emotions, and failing to do this causes further stress on our mental, emotional, spiritual, and physical health.

It's also important to know that grieving and working through the loss does not damage our Christian testimony or diminish our faith in God. In fact, sharing our heartache with the Lord will build our relationship with him and will help our faith grow as we depend on him to heal our brokenness.

Another Christian myth is that we should only express joy when we pray. But who better than our Father in heaven knows the anguish of losing a loved one, for his own Son died at Calvary. And our Savior was known as "a man of sorrows . . . acquainted with grief" (Isaiah 53:3). When C. S. Lewis, a well-respected author and Christian apologist, married Joy Davidman, he knew he was marrying a woman dying of cancer. But he believed God wanted him to marry her despite her illness. After her death, he wrote these words in the midst of his grieving:

> Where is God? Go to him when your need is desperate, when all other help is in vain, and what do you find? A door slammed in your face and a sound of bolting and double bolting on the inside. After that, silence. . . . What can this mean? Why is He so present a commander in our time of prosperity and so very absent a help in time of trouble?[5]

Lewis had the courage to admit doubt, and his example encourages the bereaved not to hide behind the world's perception of grief or its views of the correct way to communicate our broken heart to God. Instead Lewis shows us that we should embrace our pain and grief in order to move beyond it, just as he himself did. Perhaps some might claim his words revealed a lack of faith, but in truth they exposed his vulnerability in an attempt to find reassurance. Not all who mourn feel this type of desperation. Some individuals report a stronger sense of God's presence following tragedy than prior to it. This clearly reveals that the grieving process is as unique and individual as the persons experiencing it.

Some people see God as one who allots pain and suffering in his children's lives that he himself does not understand. The Bible, however, provides a different view. Genesis 6:6 describes him as a God who was "grieved" in his heart. Further examples of divine pain and grief are found in the Garden of Gethsemane and then again later at the cross. Anyone who has lost a loved one has felt excruciating sorrow and pain, as did Jesus when he said to his disciples, "My soul is overwhelmed with sorrow to the point of death" (Matthew 26:38). And who in the midst of loss hasn't begged the Father in heaven, as Jesus did, "My Father, if it be possible, let this cup pass from me" (v. 39). At our darkest hour, perhaps as we stood at the grave of a child, parent, or spouse, we have probably cried, "My God, my God, why have you forsaken me?"

If Jesus is our example, we must trust that sharing our innermost pain and sorrow will bring us healing as well as deeper intimacy with God. Hiding our feelings only suppresses our ability to heal and at the same time oppresses our spirits. It is completely normal to long for that which we've lost. It reveals our Christlike nature—compassion, love, empathy, and concern for others.

When Jesus arrived in Bethany following Lazarus' death, he wept (John 11:35). Ken Gire describes this scene so beautifully in his book *Incredible Moments with the Savior*:

> On our way to Lazarus' tomb we stumble on still another question. Jesus approaches the gravesite with the full assurance that he will raise his friend from the dead. Why then does the sight of the tomb trouble him?
>
> Maybe the tomb in the garden is too graphic a reminder of Eden gone to seed. Of Paradise lost. And of the cold, dark tomb he would have to enter to regain it.
>
> In any case, it is remarkable that our plight could trouble his spirit; that our pain could summon his tears. The raising of Lazarus is the most daring and dramatic of all the Savior's healings. He courageously went into a den where hostility raged against him to snatch a friend from the jaws of death. It was an incredible moment. It revealed that Jesus was who he said he was—the resurrection and the life. But it revealed something else.
>
> The tears of God.
>
> And who's to say which is more incredible—a man who raises the dead . . . or a God who weeps.[6]

We must realize that a God who weeps, grieves, and experiences sorrow is a God who loves us so much that he subjected himself to the very essence of pain that we endure. He did this so he could take us into his arms, cradle our weak and emotionally lifeless bodies, give us new life, and nurture us back to spiritual health with the assurance that he loves us and will never forsake us.

It is unfortunate that the disciples did not come to a stage of understanding in their anticipatory grief. Instead they chose a road that led to further grief. They resisted prayer and a reliance on God for strength. As a result, they failed miserably. In the midst of our anguish we have the same choice—to cling to God for help in the deepest crevasses of our darkness or to sleep through it in an attempt to avoid certain failure. In doing the latter, we will fail when we are tested, just like those who have gone before us.

Jesus asked Martha, the sister of Lazarus, a very critical question when she argued with him about trusting him. Martha yearned for a miracle, she desired to see her brother raised from the dead, and she wanted healing from her grief, and yet she resisted Jesus' attempt to bring restoration.

> Then Jesus, deeply moved again, came to the tomb. It was a cave, and a stone lay against it. Jesus said, "Take away the stone." Martha, the sister of the dead man, said to him, "Lord, by this time there will be an odor, for he has been dead four days." Jesus said to her, "Did I not tell you that if you believed you would see the glory of God?" (John 11:38-40)

Do you want to see the glory of God? Do you desire to partake of the freedom and life offered by the only One who has the power to resurrect your broken heart from the dead, so to speak? If so, take away the stone; remove whatever barrier stands between you and him, whatever keeps you from crying out to God during this crucial moment in your life.

8

GOD'S WILL IN
THE GARDEN

"My Father, if it be possible, let this cup pass from me; nevertheless, not as I will, but as you will."

MATTHEW 26:39

When it becomes obvious that we cannot hold onto the past and must move forward, a choice must be made—God's will or our own. It only takes me a few moments to remember where my own will has taken me in life, and I quickly surrender myself to God's will, knowing full well that whatever I fear about his will in my life pales in comparison to the potential destruction my own will would bring.

Jesus fell with his face to the ground and prayed, "My Father, if it be possible, let this cup pass from me," all the while knowing it wasn't, then added, "not as I will, but as you will." It was the desire, wish, and will of Jesus to avoid the suffering at hand and for an alternative to be found to fulfill his Father's redemptive purposes. The "cup" he was about to drink not only contained suffering and death but also God's wrath. The word *cup* anticipates that which it represents. In other words, Jesus was experiencing anticipatory suffering, wrath, and death at that very moment. The anguish was beyond comprehension and would only get worse before it got better.

This scene in the Bible indicates that our Savior was not walking around with a religious smile pasted on his face, saying that he was "fine" and everything was going to be okay in just a few hours. In contrast, we believers often believe it is our role in the midst of suffering to "put on a happy face."

"Never let them see you sweat" was a popular television commercial tag line that Christians subconsciously pick up through the legalistic expectations of others and apply to their lives despite severe anguish. They paste a façade of joy over their pain, afraid that others will judge their walk with God, fearing that God will reject them if they express their heartache, and mistakenly believing there is something drastically wrong with them because they are experiencing pain.

If Jesus is our example (and he is), why do we believe foolishly that we cannot express our heartache, distress, sorrow, and torment? He did. Cursing at God is disrespectful and dishonoring, not to mention blasphemous. However, telling him how we feel and how we desire to be released of the burden we are carrying is not. Some of the Bible's greatest leaders spoke boldly to the Lord about the struggles they faced, even asking him to take their lives, and he did not punish or reject them. For example:

• Moses was consumed with the complaints of the Israelites whom he was trying to lead into the Promised Land. The burden overwhelmed him, and he felt that it was too much for him to carry. In the expression of his frustration to God he asked, "If you will treat me like this, kill me at once" (Numbers 11:11-15).

• God sent Jonah to warn the city of Nineveh that he was going to destroy them because of their wickedness. The 120,000 people repented of their sins and fasted to show God their hearts. As a result, God did not destroy the city, but Jonah became angry at God for being merciful. He was so upset that he asked God to kill him, saying, "it is better for me to die than to live." As if that weren't enough, he repeated the same request the following day (Jonah 4:1-11).

• After the prophet Elijah ordered four hundred priests of Baal to be executed, King Ahab went and told his wife, the wicked Jezebel, who wore the proverbial pants in the family, that all of her false prophets were dead. As a result, she swore to kill Elijah within twenty-four hours. Elijah fled for his life and hid in the wilderness, praying "that he might die" (1 Kings 18:40; 19:4).

Moses and Jonah weren't dealing with what we would normally consider heart-wrenching situations. Moses was overwhelmed by the people's whining, and Jonah was angry that God showed mercy to pagan enemies (although he himself had been a recipient of that same mercy). Elijah was really the only one who had a direct threat to his life. But all three did not hesitate to share their pain and frustration. We often do the same.

• "If there is any other way, Lord, than taking my child's life, I beg of you to grant it!"

• "Take my breath from me, God, so I can be with you in heaven. I can't take it anymore!"

• "Bring my husband back to me, God. I need him to help me raise our children!"

• "Heal me miraculously, Lord. I cast myself on you."

• "I don't want to live anymore, Father. Take my life."

These statements, as well as others that we may be harboring deep within us, are normal, healthy expressions of our pain. There are nine more words we need to say: "Yet not as I will, but as you will." These may be the hardest words we'll ever say, and this can only be done after we surrender our will to God's.

I SURRENDER ALL

All to Jesus, I surrender;
All to Him I freely give;
I will ever love and trust Him,
In His presence daily live.
I surrender all, I surrender all,
All to Thee, my blessed Savior,
I surrender all.
JUDSON W. VAN DEVENTER

Every time I'm praising the Lord, I try to ask myself if what I'm saying is true or a lie. We often become complacent in worship, mouthing the words of hymns and praise songs without really investing in the power of what we are speaking. I have found that it's just as easy to sing a lie as it is to tell one. And when we do not mean what we verbalize to God through worship, we defile our sacrifice of praise. I personalize every worship song I sing. It helps to close my eyes and focus on each word I'm singing to my Heavenly Father, as if each one is a fragrant offering. Despite the fact that I can't carry a tune in a bucket, I know he basks in my praise to him.

The lyrics to the song "I Surrender All" are simple but powerful. At the same time, they can be scary because the word *surrender* doesn't always have the best connotations to it. To surrender in battle is to admit defeat, to lay down your arms, and to let go of all hope of victory. Overcoming the negative implications of this word may be necessary before we can embrace it willingly.

We "surrender" every day to people and circumstances around us because, in short, we believe in the person or the purpose behind the act. We yield to another driver not only because it's the law but because we believe it will keep us safe—and out of jail! We submit to the desires of our employers because it's their business and they have veto power and because we reap the financial benefits of employment. We give in to various governing laws because we believe we can provide some stability and consistency in the world by following them and ultimately provide safety for ourselves and our families. Similarly, we must learn to surrender to God.

Learning how to surrender involves coming to an understanding of God's character and nature. In other words, we must understand to whom we are surrendering and the purpose or point behind it. Below are just a few descriptions of who God is and who he's been to me and to many others in the darkest hours.

• *Unchangeable.* Malachi 3:6 tells us, "I the LORD do not change." He is the same yesterday, today, and forever (Hebrews 13:8). I can trust that he will be as faithful today in the midst of my crisis as he was yesterday when everything was going okay.

• *Omnipresent.* In Jeremiah 23:23–24 God asks, "Am I a God at hand . . . and not a God afar off? Can a man hide himself in secret places so that I cannot see him? . . . Do I not fill heaven and earth?" No matter how small or how big my wound is in comparison to others', God is right here, right now, ready to minister to me.

• *Truthful.* God does not and will not lie to me. Hebrews 6:18 promises me that "it is impossible for God to lie." Titus 1:2 speaks of a "knowledge of the truth, which accords with godliness, in hope of eternal life, which God, who never lies, promised before the ages began." God has told us that he rewards those who diligently seek him (Hebrews 11:6). He says he will not leave us or forsake us. He says that he can and will heal us if we come to him for healing. And he will not go back on his promises.

• *Good.* Psalm 100:5 tells us, "The LORD is good; his steadfast love endures forever, and his faithfulness to all generations." God is good, and his desires for us are good as well. We know God is good to us despite what's going on around us. We can trust him although our circumstances may tell us otherwise.

• *Merciful.* We may be in misery, but Exodus 34:6 tells us that he is "merciful and gracious . . . slow to anger and abounding in steadfast love and faithfulness." He does not require us to meet a specific emotional quota before he will show us mercy. He is granting it now, if we are willing to receive it.

• *Full of grace.* When we are suffering at our own hand from sin that we committed, he is full of grace, although we do not deserve it. Romans 3:23-24 promises us, "all have sinned and fall short of the glory of God, and are justified by his grace as a gift, through the redemption that is in Christ Jesus." First Peter 5:10 promises that we will only suffer for a season, and when that time is over, our spirit will be fortified: "the God of all grace, who has called you to his eternal glory in Christ, will himself restore, confirm, strengthen, and establish you."

• *Omniscient.* Our God is all-knowing. First John 3:20 says, "God is greater than our heart, and he knows everything." Not every other thing or some things, but *everything.* He made you, and he knows exactly what it will take to heal you. Furthermore, he *is* the balm of Gilead. The healing he wants to give you will leave no scars.

When I was nineteen, I was in a horrific motorcycle accident. I passed out at the scene, and when I awoke I was in the emergency room covered head to toe with deep crevices of what is not-so-fondly referred to as "road rash." It was not a pretty picture. For months after the accident I had to sit in a large vat of warm water at the hospital to soak off the scabs that resulted from all the ripping of my flesh. Every day a nurse would come in after I'd soaked in the water for an hour or so and literally scrub the scabs off my body with a plastic scrubbing sponge. Even the heavy narcotics they gave me couldn't prevent the pain of this procedure, I assure you. After the scrubbing was completed, the nurse would apply a cream (zinc oxide) to my many wounds. I'll never forget the name because it was a crucial part of my healing. Zinc oxide is used on severe burns and wounds so there will be no scarring.

I was nineteen, unsaved, and what my mother called "buck wild." So after my release from the hospital, when the responsibility fell on me to put the cream on myself, I did so hit and miss and eventually stopped altogether. I had healed without scars over most of my body. I stopped using the zinc oxide on only two places—the places where I had been most deeply wounded—my knees. Ironically, as a believer the Lord reminds me that it is when I'm on my scarred knees that he can heal me. When I apply him (spiritual zinc oxide) to my wounds, I can experience complete healing. When I refuse, I will scar, becoming bitter and resentful. The same is true for you.

To heal our pain and anguish we often go to the world's medicine cabinet. We go to counseling, read self-help books on various topics, and seek the advice of others. But these are merely Band-Aids for a dying world. They cover the wound, but the wound only heals on the surface, continuing to fester underneath. The Bible reveals both man's way of change and God's. Let's look at the difference.

GOD'S GIFT OF HEALING VS. MAN'S WAY

In biblical times four stages of life were observed—birth, maturity, marriage, and death. While these events record the external progressions of life, there is a far more critical area to consider—the internal and spiritual growth and healing process, sometimes called *metamorphosis*. To understand this Greek word's true meaning, we need to look at it in two parts. *Meta* primarily means "with, in the midst of, or among," and in John 3:2 it refers to God's helping hand or presence in ministry. *Morphosis* (or *morphe*) means "to form, transform, or alter fundamentally." These two words together describe the changes that a human passes through in his or her growth from conception (egg) to maturity (adulthood) in the presence of God. The English word *morph* comes from the Greek word *morphoo*, which means "the inward and real formation of the essential nature of a person." This term is used to describe the formation and growth of an embryo in a mother's body or the work of artists who shape their material into an image. In the New Testament *morphoo* is found only in Galatians 4:19, where the Christian is described as a little child who needs to mature until the very image of Christ is impressed upon his or her heart. It is interesting to note that *morphoo* involves a change that occurs from the inside out. Any real change or healing in one's life must happen internally.

The word *metamorphosis* is also used to describe Jesus' transfiguration (Matthew 17:2; Mark 9:2), which involved the miracle of transformation from an earthly form into a supernatural one. Thus metamorphosis can be a spiritual transformation, an invisible process that takes place within the hearts of Christians (see Romans 12:2; 2 Corinthians 3:18).

Often when we hear the word *metamorphosis*, we think of an insect—specifically the butterfly, who evolves from an egg to larva to pupa and then into adulthood. Entomologists, scientists who specialize in the study of insects, recognize two basic forms of metamorphosis—complete and incomplete. In the *complete* form, an insect travels through all stages of growth, starting with conception, moving on into adulthood, and finally becoming a butterfly. During this process it is not unusual for an insect to undergo multiple changes in physical form—both inside and out, but initially always from within. In a complete metamorphosis the function of the newborn insect is to eat and grow until it becomes an adult and can reproduce. In an *incomplete* metamorphosis, the insect develops only partially, never realizing its full potential.

Extending this metaphor to Christianity can be helpful. Without Christ as our Savior, we can never develop to our full potential because that cannot happen unless and until we change into the image of Christ, and we can't do that if our sins are not covered by the blood he shed for us on the cross. Further, apart from the blood of Jesus we cannot experience complete healing in any area of our lives.

There is a parallel biblical comparison to incomplete metamorphosis as seen in the Greek word *metaschematizo*, which means "to change one's outward form." *Metaschematizo*, however, does not alter a person internally. The *Key Word Study Bible* describes the difference between *metamorphoo* and *metaschematizo* in this way:

> If one were to change a Dutch garden into an Italian one, this would be *metaschematizo*. But if one were to transform a garden into something wholly different, as into a baseball field, it is *metamorphoo*—to change in complete form.[7]

Metaschematizo is often observed in modern medicine's approach to healing. Many tools, techniques, and books utilized for the purpose of healing and transformation merely cover the wound, which only heals on the surface. Complete and perfect healing of the soul, as well as transformation, comes only from one place—the cross of Jesus Christ.

I spent years in therapy as a result of childhood abuse and self-inflicted abuse as an adolescent and young adult. I've read many self-help books and have attended hundreds of secular seminars on how to attain healing, peace, and joy. I even studied child psychology in an attempt to figure myself out! In doing so, I eventually functioned in a somewhat healthy manner in a dysfunctional world. Nothing I tried, however, brought anything near complete healing in any area of my life. Metaphorically speaking, I moved from a Dutch garden to an Italian garden, but I sensed I needed something more—I just didn't know what.

When I became a believer on November 2, 1993, construction began from within and continues today, transforming a garden overrun by weeds into a temple where the Holy Spirit resides. Although the remodeling is not yet complete, the Holy Spirit is the contractor who oversees every step of the building process. The goal is that the temple within will ultimately reflect the image of Christ, something that God himself will accomplish (Romans 8:29).

Suffering requires a process of healing that can only be attained in complete metamorphosis in Christ. It is impossible to evolve into the image of Jesus apart from struggle because we must share in his suffering to become like him in image. Let me give you another fascinating lesson about the transformation that occurs in the life of a butterfly in relation to the believer.

A caterpillar faces a big challenge as it grows and matures into a butterfly. It must make new, larger skin and goes through several moltings to generate new skin to make room for its growing body. In the final stage the caterpillar forms a chrysalis, an outer shell to protect the final process of transformation into the end product.

Many people think this is a nap time or a rest period for the caterpillar, but this is definitely not so. It's a critical time of necessary and severe struggling for the new creature. Life and death weigh in the balance during this last transition. The body of the caterpillar is transforming into an adult butterfly, and any interruption in the process is sure to bring sudden death.

When the butterfly emerges from the chrysalis approximately two weeks later, its wings are small and moist, and it cannot fly yet. The new creature, in its adult-infant stage of transformation, must pump blood from its abdomen through the veins in its wings, which causes the wings to expand to their full size. The blood pumped to the wings brings new life. If this process is interfered with or interrupted in any way, that will cause arrested development, preventing the butterfly from maturing to its full capacity, and it will promptly die. Though designed by God to fly, bring joy to all who see it, reproduce, and proclaim God's grace and goodness, such a butterfly is incapable of carrying out its God-given role.

Similarly, as believers the process of becoming a new creation in Christ requires moving away from our old nature and from a dependence on self, others, and the world to heal and mature us. We do this by allowing the blood of Jesus to pump through our spirit, bringing life to us. Anytime we allow the world to interfere with the process by interjecting its ways, we invite spiritual ruin. We are most frail, most vulnerable, when we are learning to allow the blood of Jesus to soothe our wounds and rule our lives. Only the Creator of the universe has hands gentle enough, a heart patient enough, and the incredible amount of love needed to apply the healing balm of Gilead. But when he is through, we will fly, we will be free, and we will no longer have any scars.

9

Betrayed with a Kiss

*Now the betrayer had given them a sign, saying, "The one I will kiss
is the man; seize him." And he came up to Jesus at once and said,
"Greetings, Rabbi!" And he kissed him.*

MATTHEW 26:48-49

When I married him, I was convinced I was marrying my best
friend, my soul mate, the love of my life. On paper everything
looked perfect. He was in ministry, and so was I. We had both been
through our share of ups and downs and had persevered, and we agreed
we could do more for God together than we could do individually. But I
was wrong—horribly wrong and potentially *gravely* wrong.

"He's going to kill you," my spiritual mentor and confidante, Betty,
would say to me on the phone a thousand miles away time and time
again over the following three years. "You have to leave him."

"I can't," I'd sob. "I love him."

"Abuse is not love, Les. Can't you see? You're acting out the same
part as you did in the childhood script that you played with your bio-
logical father. You're trying to say and do whatever is needed to be perfect, so you can earn his love. But, Les, he's not capable of loving you
because of his own issues."

She was right *every time* she said it. I'd married my abusive father,
only worse. I believed I was spiritually bound to him and could never
escape. Physical abuse, pornography, other women, and subtle words of
defeat that he threw at me again and again were all damaging, but spiri-

tual abuse and the misuse and twisting of Scripture kept me bound to shame, self-hatred, and ultimately to him.

"God hates divorce," he'd say over and over, knowing he'd broken the marital covenant and wasn't walking righteously before the Lord. "I wouldn't have to slap you if you were more submissive," he'd shout as the sting of his hand swelled my cheek. "Quit being so rebellious," he'd insist as I resisted him as he forced me facedown into a pillow where I'd have to struggle for breath. "Women are to be silent," he'd say as he clenched his hand tightly over my jaw, squeezing forcefully. "If I want your opinion, I'll ask for it." But the most damaging words, the ones that shook the very essence of my being and took me right back to my childhood and my father, were, "You make it impossible to love you!"

So I'd try to be more submissive and more accommodating. I'd speak only when spoken to and would walk on eggshells just to please him. I'd fast and pray that the Lord would change my rebellious heart and restore my husband's love for me. And when the Holy Spirit revealed to me that my husband was not being faithful and he adamantly denied it, I believed *him* instead of God.

"The Holy Spirit didn't tell you that," he'd lie. "You're speaking out of your own insecurity."

I'd feel ashamed of my confronting him and would apologize profusely. But that was part of his manipulation and control, designed to shift my dependence from God to him, and it worked. I lived and breathed for him only and hung on every word he spoke, hoping for a morsel of love and acceptance. In the meantime, if he said I was wrong, unlovable, unattractive, or ungodly, I believed it. Slowly but surely the voice of the Holy Spirit inside me became harder to hear, and I became confused. Without even recognizing what was happening, I changed my allegiance from Jesus Christ to my husband. He had become my "savior."

Three years later, after I had suffered a fractured back and immeasurable amounts of physical abuse, spiritual and mental brainwashing, and endless emotional manipulation, my "savior" was going to jail for two and a half years for domestic violence, and I was left alone, unable to sift through the ruins of my life.

It has taken more than four years to work through the pain and anguish I experienced in that relationship. For the first eighteen months I didn't think I would survive. I was solemnly and chronically depressed, I lost fifty pounds, I cried continually, and I withdrew from everyone and everything. I had become an empty shell during my marriage, void of purpose and hope, having lost the recognition of the identity in Christ to which I had once clung. The light of Jesus that formerly shined so brightly within me and my ministry had not only dimmed to a mere flicker during our marriage but had eventually disappeared entirely. How could I ever get my faith in God back?

"The greatest wound you'll ever experience in life," the man who led me to the Lord told me the day I gave my life to Jesus, "will be from another believer." I hadn't fully understood what he meant when he said that, but I understood his words all too well later as I grappled with the sorrow of my broken marriage. It was an especially deep wound because it was made by someone close to me—my confidant, my friend, my lover, one whom I'd hoped would be my partner throughout my life—the one who was called to honor and cherish me and to love me sacrificially. I believe that Jesus felt similarly deep and painful disappointment when his beloved disciple, a man he'd chosen to serve alongside him, in essence a brother, betrayed him for a mere thirty pieces of silver.

A Prophecy of Betrayal

"Truly, I say to you, one of you will betray me" (Matthew 26:21). Can you imagine how shocking those words must have sounded to the twelve disciples as they shared the Passover meal with Jesus? Silence must have permeated the room. Undoubtedly everyone stopped eating, wiped their mouths on the sleeves of their tunics, had trouble swallowing their last bite of roasted lamb, and felt pressure well up in their chests from the penetrating truth of Jesus' prophecy of disloyalty. Verse 22 tells us they were grieved by his words, and as the truth sank into their hearts, they each asked, "Is it I, Lord?"

A traitor sat with the Savior of the world. Not all of the men partaking of the Lord's Supper were holy. They were not all believers or sincere servants of Christ. Jesus made the point that his betrayer would be a friend, someone close to and intimate with him, someone breaking bread with him at that very moment in time, thus heightening the enormity of the infidelity. At that point Jesus silenced the questions and arrested the fear that arose in the other eleven men by identifying the perpetrator and untrustworthy disciple specifically as "he who has dipped his hand in the dish with me" (v. 23).

The spotlight on the stage of Christ's predestined crucifixion shone brightly onto Judas, brutally exposing his unfaithful heart. To be silent would only entrap him further. No doubt he felt forced to speak up. "Is it I, Rabbi?" he asked (v. 25).

Jesus' response was affirmative, leaving no room for doubt, and yet without apology or blame. "Yes, it is you" (v. 25, NIV).

I can only imagine the array of emotions that Jesus' words provoked in Judas, and the extraordinary relief within the hearts of the others at the table. The Gospel of Matthew tells us that the disciples carried on with their Passover meal, at which point Jesus initiated the first Communion ceremony ever.

After confronting his betrayer, Jesus did what seems absurd—he took an unleavened loaf, gave thanks, broke it, distributed it, and said, "Take, eat; this is my body" (v. 26).

"Wait a minute, Jesus," everything inside me wants to scream. "Do something! Ask Judas to leave the table! Curse him! Take his breath away from him so he cannot harm you or anyone else! It doesn't make sense to dine with the enemy! Send him away!" But the Savior didn't do that. Instead, sacrificial overtones were clear in his gift of Communion. Through his body about to be broken, his life about to be given for us all, Jesus was offering the disciples, including the one who would initiate the violent breaking of his body, reconciliation with God.

After they had all partaken of the bread as symbolic of his body, Jesus held up a cup and commanded *all* of the disciples to drink from it, signifying the blood that he would shed on their behalf and on behalf of all sinners. At any moment after Jesus confronted him about his upcoming betrayal, Judas could have confessed the sin in his heart and sought forgiveness, but he didn't. He partook of the offering at hand, sang intimate praises with and to the Son of Man he was about to turn over to authorities to be brutally tortured and killed, and later approached him in the Garden and greeted him with a kiss, as though he were Jesus' friend.

Perhaps you too have had a "friend" such as this—someone in your inner circle who has betrayed you—a mate, child, parent, coworker, sibling, or business partner. You never believed the betrayal would occur. It hit you from out of nowhere, blindsiding you from left field. The shock itself was enough to knock you off your feet, and much more pain followed. You thought you knew the other person better than that. You thought you could trust, depend on, and confide in him or her. He or she claimed to be part of the Body of Christ, but now you question the sincerity of his or her spiritual walk.

The harsh reality, as we see in the Lord's Supper on the eve of Christ's betrayal and in the men sitting around that table, is that evil and good are found side by side; the wheat and the tares will grow together until the harvest. However, having that knowledge does not make it easier to digest the heartache of betrayal.

When harmed by another person who claims to know Christ, we are typically left with even more pain than at the hand of an unbeliever. We naturally wonder how someone who professes Jesus as his or her Savior could have done such a thing. We expect nonbelievers to act like sinners, but we hold believers to a higher standard. Judas was one of the Twelve. No one would have expected him to turn against Jesus like he did. How could someone walk with the Son of God every day for over three years, personally observing miracles, hearing the truth in everything Jesus said, being mentored by the promised Messiah, and share an intimacy that few others have ever experienced on a one-on-one basis, then betray him so callously?

Of course, Judas wouldn't be the only disciple to betray Jesus. As a matter of fact, Jesus made it clear that all twelve men would fail him. He said, "You will all fall away because of me this night. For it is written, 'I will strike the shepherd, and the sheep of the flock will be scattered'" (Matthew 26:31, quoting Zechariah 13:7). The disciples did not appreciate their Savior's honesty, and Peter immediately responded, "Though they all fall away because of you, I will never fall away." Sadly, a well-intentioned heart does not necessarily make a faithful one. Jesus replied to Peter, "Truly, I tell you, this very night, before the rooster crows, you will deny me three times." But Peter insisted he would not fall, and all the disciples said the same (Matthew 26:33-35). When they did desert him, they were so upset, they didn't even remember Jesus' prophecy about the resurrection.

Can you imagine not just one of your closest friends betraying you and letting you down but *twelve* of them, and all on the same night? Jesus was heartbroken, I assure you, by the abandonment of his closest followers. But he also knew that he fought not against flesh and blood but against his greatest enemy, Satan (see Ephesians 6:12), and this made the battle even more fierce.

THE ROLE OF SATAN IN SUFFERING

Judas was a pawn in the hand of Satan until the night of Jesus' arrest when Scripture tells us the enemy actually entered him (Luke 22:3; John 13:27). In considering the heart of those who betrayed us, we must understand that we are all susceptible to being used by the Devil through the flesh. Scripture clearly refers to this process in James 1:14-15: "Each person is tempted when he is lured and enticed by his own desire. Then desire when it has conceived gives birth to sin, and sin when it is fully grown brings forth death."

When our heart is bent on fulfilling our own desires, and we do not submit to the Word of God, we too become tools in the hand of the Evil One. Thus we all betray Jesus at one time or another. However, like Judas, we can choose to repent and turn our hearts back to our First Love, a divine offer he refused.

At first Judas was only a receptive vessel being used by Satan to set a trap. He was not initially possessed by Satan. Possession implies ownership, and had Judas made a profession of faith and received Jesus Christ as his Savior, he would have become the property of God. Scripture tells us that when we accept Jesus into our hearts, we are bought with a price (1 Corinthians 6:19-20). Satan cannot enter or take ownership of someone who belongs to God. Nor can he snatch someone out of the hands of God (John 10:28-29). An important point to make here is that Judas was receptive to evil because his heart was hardened toward the truth.

On an occasion well before his final trip to Jerusalem, Jesus stated that he specifically chose the twelve disciples though he knew that one of them was "a devil" (John 6:70-71). The Greek word translated "devil" here means "malicious, slanderous," implying that Judas had an evil nature. His heart was bent on evil instead of on good, as we see in his "fruit" less than a week before Jesus' arrest in the Garden.

On that earlier occasion in the village of Bethany, Judas' true heart was exposed (John 12:8). After Mary anointed Christ's feet with expensive spikenard and wiped his feet with her hair, Judas asked Jesus why the ointment was wasted on him rather than being sold and the money given to the poor. His question revealed the worthlessness of Jesus and his ministry from that perpetrator's perspective. After serving beside Jesus for years, he had totally missed the point: Jesus is the Son of God, and there never will be enough expensive perfume in the world to show his true worth. Perpetrators like Judas never see value in Jesus or even in others.

In response to his foolishness, Jesus rebuked Judas, knowing that he didn't care about the poor but was a thief. As the one who kept the money box, Judas just wanted to have more money to steal for himself. Judas was a hard-hearted man, a narcissist whose apparent concern for others was in actuality motivated by his own greed.

Then in Luke 22 we find Satan actually physically entering Judas, possessing him entirely:

> *Then Satan entered into Judas called Iscariot, who was of the number of the twelve. He went away and conferred with the chief priests and officers how he might betray him to them. And they were glad, and agreed to give him money. So he consented and sought an opportunity to betray him to them in the absence of a crowd. (vv. 3-6)*

Jesus referred to Judas as "the son of perdition" (John 17:12, NKJV). As horrific as it is to be considered a traitor or betrayer in general, both of those labels pale in comparison to being referred to as "the son of perdition." The name denotes that Judas was a man identified with eternal destruction, one whose destiny was the Lake of Fire, hell. So we see that there was a drastic change in Judas. At one point he was merely a vessel of the Devil; later he was no longer his own but was possessed by the Evil One. To understand the role of Satan in suffering, we must be able to look at the difference between our adversary being a tool and his or her being held under the total sway of the enemy. Let me explain why that's important.

After my husband went to jail and I began divorce proceedings, many well-intentioned believers proclaimed that he was unsaved, some even proclaiming he was possessed. After all, how could someone who had accepted Jesus into his heart act in such a way?

As with other believers who have harmed me (consciously or unconsciously), my husband had some incredible gifts in the Lord. I saw him minister to some people effectively in Christ at times. But some of the most gifted people in the Body of Christ have detrimental strongholds that far outshadow their gifts in the Lord. Such was the case with my husband. Even as I look over my own walk, I can see where I have hurt other people over the years. As I mentioned previously, wounded people wound people, and because we are all wounded by sin, we all wound others at some point. This is not said to make excuses for hurtful behavior or to claim that our perpetrators certainly have redemption, but I will say that spending an excessive amount of time debating whether or not the one who has wounded you is saved is not beneficial to your own walk.

It matters little, in the wake of pain and anguish, whether or not the perpetrator is saved. The damage has been done to you. Trying to justify it by saying the other person was not a believer in no way lessens the pain or glorifies God. While we can (and should) pray for all who have harmed us, we must move forward, leaving the perpetrators in the care of Jesus, who so adequately, without sin, judgment, retaliation, or prejudice, can deal with them, offering them the gift of forgiveness that we may not be ready or willing to extend. Instead, let us look into our own hearts and leave others to answer for themselves to God, remembering that we also are not without sin.

Regardless of where the human being who has harmed us stands in his or her spiritual state, we are told in Ephesians 6 that we do not fight against flesh and blood. Satan himself is our greatest enemy. He therefore is the one against whom we war. The friend who carelessly revealed a confidence, the mate who left you for another, the trusted adult who took advantage of your innocence during your childhood, or the employee who stole from you were all pawns, as was Judas in the plan to kill Jesus. The reason the enemy chose someone within your immediate circle to harm you is because only a trusted friend or family member can betray you; a stranger cannot. You can only be betrayed by someone you have allowed into your heart.

When a family member, trusted friend, or confidant becomes a traitor, the betrayal cuts so deeply that healing is almost impossible. Without spiritual intervention, this can lead to feelings of bitterness, emotional withdrawal, fear, and an inability to accept love from others in the future. We must keep in mind that Satan's purpose is to steal, kill, and destroy (John 10:10).

SPIRITUAL WARFARE AND SUFFERING

The believer is at war, and God has given the believer all the ability, strength, and power of heaven to fight against Satan and his cohorts. The same power that raised Jesus from the dead lives within us (Ephesians 1:19-20). But it is up to us to access it. We do so by learning God's Word, spending time with him, allowing the Holy Spirit to be our instructor, and exercising our faith. We also do this by taking every thought captive to the obedience of Jesus Christ (2 Corinthians 10:4-5).

One way the enemy of our souls assaults the wounded is by dropping suggestive thoughts into their minds. These mind-grenades usually fall right into a tender wound, feeding already existing unhealthy beliefs. In my darkest hours I often battled the thought that God didn't care about me or my circumstances. If he did, he'd intervene. That was a lie that I nurtured at times. God did care and was intervening, just not in the way that I wanted or demanded. When I didn't take that thought captive, I found myself avoiding time alone with him. I became angry, depressed, and bitter. I resisted intimacy and time in the Word. But as I learned to take thoughts captive to the truth, I noticed a very different outcome to my sorrow. This procedure is referred to as the cognitive process, and I outline it in great detail in my book *Engaging the Enemy* (Cook Communication Ministries, 2006).

We are all in a spiritual battle, from the day we are born until the day we die. If you have not received Jesus as your Savior, you are property yet to be purchased, and you are being courted by the kingdom of hell and by the kingdom of heaven. Your choice will determine the final outcome of your suffering and where you will spend eternity. If you have accepted Christ's sacrifice as payment for your sins, Satan's desire is to draw your eyes away from your First Love. He will do that by dropping thought-grenades about how unfaithful God is to you during your trials. You must not give the enemy an inch in your mind, for he will take a mile and then some!

Your greatest battle will be done on the front lines of your mind during this time of your life when you are facing great difficulty. Be prepared to stand against the lies of the enemy that will inevitably assault you. Standing on God's Word will give you the strength to take the necessary steps for you to walk through healing, which we will examine later. But first we will consider another aspect of spiritual warfare for those who are suffering—taking time daily to flank oneself in the armor of God.

THE ARMOR OF GOD

In reading through Ephesians 6 we can almost hear the war trumpet sound. That strategic passage tells us to put on armor so we can be strong against the Devil's schemes. Those of us who are wounded by life's circumstances can be even more susceptible to injuries from the enemy. Satan always goes for the wounded first. He sees them as weak, easy targets. It's especially important at such a time to protect ourselves by wearing the armor of God. The apostle Paul, a man familiar with suffering himself, instructs believers on how to prepare themselves in verses 10-20:

> *Finally, be strong in the Lord and in the strength of his might. Put on the whole armor of God, that you may be able to stand against the schemes of the devil. For we do not wrestle against flesh and blood, but against the rulers, against the authorities, against the cosmic powers over this present darkness, against the spiritual forces of evil in the heavenly places. Therefore take up the whole armor of God, that you may be able to withstand in the evil day, and having done all, to stand firm. Stand therefore, having fastened on the belt of truth, and having put on the breastplate of*

righteousness, and, as shoes for your feet, having put on the readiness given by the gospel of peace. In all circumstances take up the shield of faith, with which you can extinguish all the flaming darts of the evil one; and take the helmet of salvation, and the sword of the Spirit, which is the word of God, praying at all times in the Spirit, with all prayer and supplication. To that end keep alert with all perseverance, making supplication for all the saints, and also for me, that words may be given to me in opening my mouth boldly to proclaim the mystery of the gospel, for which I am an ambassador in chains, that I may declare it boldly, as I ought to speak.

Paul tells us to "be strong in the Lord and in the strength of his might." Thus we must draw all the resources we need from Christ and his mighty power. The Greek word for Christ's power here is *kratos*, the same word used for the power that raised Jesus from the dead and for the power that brought us to life in Christ when we were dead in our trespasses and sins. It means "to take hold of, grasp, have power over, hold in one's hand." It is a proclamation that we are not alone, that Christ is with us, that we have the power of Christ at hand. We can, therefore, be strong in his power, knowing that we do not fight the battle alone.

Paul also told us to "put on the whole armor of God, that you may be able to stand against the schemes of the devil." One of the most wonderful things about our spiritual armor is that the Bible describes God as wearing the very same pieces of armor. Isaiah 11:5 tells us that righteousness and faithfulness make up the Messiah's belt around his waist. Isaiah 59:17 tells us that righteousness is also his breastplate, that he wears the helmet of salvation on his head, and that he wears the garments of vengeance and wraps himself in zeal as his cloak. What an honor it is to dress ourselves in armor similar to that of our Commander! Our Father knew that every part of our bodies, from head to foot, must be protected. So he created various pieces of armor for our use.

The items of the armor appear in the order in which they should be put on as we prepare for battle. Once the armor is on, it leaves no place on our body uncovered.

First, we are to gird our waists with "truth" (Ephesians 6:14). "Truth" in this verse represents both the truth of the gospel and the truth within us. In biblical battles the belt was crucial because it kept the breastplate in place. Additionally, the sword hung from the belt and needed to be held securely there for easy retrieval. When the warrior wore his belt, it indicated that he was prepared to see action. He loosened it only when he was off duty.

In biblical times, the waist or abdominal area represented the seat of the emotions. To gird this area with truth is to commit your emotions to believing the truth. We must maintain commitment to truth regardless of the repercussions. Standing for truth often hurts other people's feelings. That can sometimes be heart-wrenching, but when there is a choice between pleasing others or pleasing God, we must always give our Creator first priority.

When we are enduring a crisis, our emotions can be the one thing that can keep us in agony. Our emotions are the by-products of our thoughts. We must hold our thoughts captive to the truth in God's Word, which will inevitably hold our emotions in check.

Second, we are to put on "the breastplate of righteousness" (Ephesians 6:14). The breastplate covered a soldier's body from the neck to the thighs and covered both his front and his back. "Righteousness" represents integrity of character.

When we wear the breastplate of righteousness, we deal fairly with others because we are using a biblical standard. We live life aboveboard; our actions match our words. We are people of character; we deal honestly, using justice and knowledge.

Once the breastplate has been fitted into position, we must prepare our feet with "the gospel of peace" (Ephesians 6:15). In biblical history, preparing one's feet for war was vital because the terrain one would encounter was often uncertain. It was the one piece of armor that a soldier could not go without, because if his feet were not shod he was limited in his mobility.

The military success of Alexander the Great is said to be in large part the result of his army being well shod and able to make long marches at incredible speed over rough terrain. In the same way, when believers are about their Father's business, ready to go anyplace to spread the gospel of peace and reconciliation, they need to prepare their feet for the journey.

In addition, we are to "take up the shield of faith" (Ephesians 6:16). The shield of the Roman soldier was generally large and oblong. It consisted of two layers of wood glued together and covered with linen and hide, which they would saturate with water and bind with iron. A soldier's shield provided excellent protection, especially when he fought side by side with his fellow soldiers, presenting a solid wall of shields to the enemy.

When we believe what God's Word says and trust what he says to be true, we can step out in faith against all the fiery darts that the enemy shoots our way.

In ancient warfare arrows or darts were often dipped in pitch and then ignited to serve as deadly incendiary weapons. Our shield of faith does not simply deflect such missiles but actually quenches the flames to prevent them from spreading. The fiery darts of the Wicked One are often doubt, fear, shame, guilt, and legalism, but the God of Truth enables us to stand and deflect them (see Hebrews 11:6).

Two more items remain—"the helmet of salvation" and "the sword of the Spirit."

The soldier's helmet covered his head and was most commonly made of bronze, with leather attachments. Putting on "the helmet of salvation" (Ephesians 6:17) protects the head, and in the spiritual sense the mind. When our heads are not covered, any number of thoughts can assault our minds and lead us off course, as we have seen. I have seen many casualties of war in this area in the matter of the assurance of salvation. The Devil puts doubt and insecurity into the minds of believers, and because their heads are not covered with the helmet of salvation, they begin to doubt the side to which they belong. This is what we call brainwashing today. If the enemy can get into the soldier's head and reprogram his thought process, he can cause devastation.

The last piece of armor that we are told to put on is "the sword of the Spirit, which is the word of God" (Ephesians 6:17). It is the only offensive weapon in the armor. Luke 4 tells us that when Jesus was combating Satan, he refuted the father of lies with the truth of God's Word.

The Word of God is powerful, effective, instructive, and razor-sharp (see Hebrews 4:12; 2 Timothy 3:16-17). It is not *our* sword, but the sword of the Spirit of God who resides in us. Knowing the power that we have within us will enable us to fight the battle at hand with confidence and strength.

Finally, we are told to pray always (see Ephesians 6:18). Prayer is a channel of communication between us and God. In the midst of battle, we as believers must stay in constant contact with our Leader for directions and encouragement. Our prayers for one another are important and effective (see James 5:16), and we must never believe the lie that God does not hear or answer our prayers.

When we pray, God makes us alert to what is happening around us. When we pray, the Spirit of God teaches us, leads us, and reveals to us the strategies of the enemy. Many people have difficulty praying because they have failed to put on the armor first. Our flesh doesn't want to pray. Neither does the enemy want us to pray because he understands the power that is available to us when we call on the God of creation.

Without God's truth, the righteousness of Christ, the gospel of peace, faith, salvation, and the sword of the Spirit, we are not motivated to pray; we just want to fulfill the desires of the flesh. In this state we become vulnerable to the enemy's taunting, and we become more susceptible to sin.

As we put the armor of the Lord on daily, we need to consider where in our lives, since we've put the armor on previously, we have sinned in that respective area. For example, we cannot put on the breastplate of righteousness without first considering where in life we have been unrighteous. The same is true with the belt of truth and the other pieces of the armor. Where have we not been truthful or have not accepted truth into our hearts? We cannot put truth on top of a lie. We must first remove the lie, exposing the untruth, then place the truth in its place. This is the most vital part of this process because it instigates the process of repentance and healing. If we find ourselves reluctant to look at a specific area of our heart or to put the armor on, there is a reason for that. We must not hide our sin and run from God, or healing will not come. Rather, let us go boldly to the throne room and confess our sin, put on the armor, and prepare to walk in victory and healing.

Walking Through Healing

Sometimes the healing of a wound can be more painful than the offense that caused it. Many people resist the healing process because of the pain that is associated with it. After all, being betrayed is hard enough, but having to face it a second time can seem unbearable. And indeed it will be unless you give it to Jesus.

One of the first steps toward healing from betrayal is *understanding* both sides of sin, as the victim and as the perpetrator of sin. Consider this: rejection, duplicity, unfaithfulness, and betrayal are all things we do to Christ when we sin and things others do to us when we are sinned against. When we finally grasp the truth that we are not unlike Judas or the other disciples and that we too have turned our back on God through our own sin, then we are able to see our betrayer in a much different light—as a sinner whom God holds accountable but to whom he also wants to show mercy, just as he has done for us.

If the person who hurt you is an unbeliever, this is no excuse to withhold forgiveness. His inability to understand God's ways does not release you from your responsibility as a Christian to forgive just as you have been forgiven. But be sure to keep this in mind: many people believe that if they let go of an offense against someone, they are in essence signaling acceptance of the transgression. This is not true. Forgiving someone means you are regaining control of your life by releasing that person from his or her sin against you and leaving him or her in the hands of God, just as Jesus did. This is a free gift; it can't be earned. But forgiving someone does not mean you must subject yourself to his or her betrayal a second time. The Lord admonishes us to be wise, and nowhere in Scripture are believers asked to be doormats. If the other party is unrepentant, do not subject yourself to continued abuse simply because you've begun the process of forgiveness.

The next step is to *take your grieving heart to the foot of the cross* for healing. Depending on the depth of the betrayal, you may have to repeat this several times. As a victim of childhood sexual abuse, it took me years to work through the betrayal of the trusted adults who assaulted me. The reason for this is because betrayal of any kind can affect multiple areas of your life—emotional, mental, physical, and even spiritual. There are many facets to the healing process.

Tell God how this betrayal has hurt you. David, who wrote most of the Psalms, is an excellent example of how to share both tragedies and triumphs with God. He spoke freely, without reservation, and was called "a man after God's own heart." Throughout Scripture God is shown as a compassionate, loving Father who wants to heal our wounds and provide comfort in the midst of healing. My favorite verses in this regard are Jeremiah 29:12-13 and Joel 2:25. He already knows what's in your heart, but sharing it with him frees you from the bondage of betrayal. Once this is accomplished, accept God's unconditional love and healing.

Next, *try not to replay the offense in your mind.* In doing so, we re-traumatize ourselves. Additionally, realize that it's not your responsibility to figure out why the person did what he or she did. I spent a lot of wasted hours trying to figure out how and why my husband became so abusive. Was it because of his childhood, external influences, or something traumatic that had happened to him? One day the Lord told me that if I spent as much time working on healing the offense as I did on figuring out why it happened, I'd be healed already! It is virtually impossible to figure out the intricate details of someone else's reasoning skills and motives. We are each the only person we can work on, and we are better off if we focus on the only one we have the ability to change, with God's help.

10

RETALIATION IN THE
GARDEN

And when those who were around him saw what would follow, they said, "Lord, shall we strike with the sword?" And one of them struck the servant of the high priest and cut off his right ear.

LUKE 22:49-50

Revenge, retaliation, vengeance, retribution, payback, punishment, reckoning, justice, settling the score, and reprisal all describe Simon Peter's response to the armed men who came forward to seize Jesus. I think he pulled out his sword and cut off the right ear of Malchus, the servant of the high priest, out of fear for his own life and out of a misguided love and devotion to Jesus.

Peter was the impulsive one of the group, always quick to speak and respond. Judging by several events in his life recorded in Scripture, his personal life motto seemed to be, "Respond now; sift through the aftermath later." He is the only disciple depicted as verbally and adamantly denying Christ after proclaiming he'd die before he would do such a thing (Matthew 26:35). He obstinately refused to allow Jesus to wash his feet (John 13:8). He rebuked Jesus harshly when he spoke of his impending death (Matthew 16:21-22). He challenged Jesus to prove his identity (Matthew 14:28). And on a whim he offered to build shelters for Jesus, Moses, and Elijah, putting them on an equal level (Matthew 17:4).

Peter is one of the most fleshed-out characters of the Bible, one whose life and mistakes are described extensively and in detail. However, Peter's failings are not presented in Scripture as hopelessly evil or heinous but as symptoms of man's sinful nature that can be overcome through faith. And that's exactly what happened with this pliable man's heart. The Book of Acts portrays Peter as a model disciple for others to emulate. As he matured in his faith, he continued to turn his heart away from his sin nature and more toward Christ and became the "rock" that Jesus prophesied he would become (the names Cephas and Peter both mean "rock"; see John 1:42).

Like Peter, we all have character flaws because we too have a sin nature. Our flesh tells us that when someone has harmed or threatened us, we need to get back at them, harm them, take something of value away from them, punish them. That sin nature shows itself early in our lives, even in babies. At the time of this writing, my grandsons Jonathan and Dallin are three years and eighteen months old respectively. When they play together and one is playing with the prized toy of the moment and the other takes it, the victim of the crime pushes the other as if to say, "Give me my toy!" The natural response of the other boy is to push back. As a result, the battle soon becomes an all-out wrestling match. Such impulses are part of our fallen nature.

I observed a similar situation recently while baby-sitting my niece and nephew. I was getting ready to do some face painting. In the process of trying to move closer to me, my nephew accidentally stepped on my niece's foot. In response, she picked up her foot and purposely stomped on my nephew's foot, at which point I had two angry and crying kids to deal with.

Sadly, we adults aren't much better. We are a lot like children when it comes to revenge. Change the toy in the first example into a prized position at your company that two people are vying for (a corner office or a promotion or a convenient parking space), or change the foot incident into a crowded freeway with two drivers at the five o'clock rush hour trying to get home, and we see adults who behave just like those children. Raise the ante by throwing adultery, murder, or money into the mix, and the stakes escalate and retaliation is angrily justified.

Long before I was writing my own books, I ghostwrote for a prominent Christian author for a couple of years. He always had difficulty paying me (and others) for my services because of his own financial problems. Despite his history, I agreed to write three books for him in exchange for a modest sum of money. To make a long story short, he never paid me for writing them, although I delivered them to him and to the publisher on the agreed date. I was livid to say the least. I'd invested a lot of time, energy, and even money in the projects, and he had no regard for my efforts. Needless to say, I never wrote for him again. But for a long time, years really, I struggled with wanting to get revenge. Day and night I thought about ways I could get back at this person. My pain was emphasized by others' account that he'd done similar things to them.

Somebody should do something! I thought to myself, naturally thinking I should be that person. But a very wise person, someone much smarter and more spiritually mature than me, challenged me to look at the motives behind my desire. I was acting just like my niece had. I wanted to hurt that man because he'd hurt me first. I'm not talking justice here—I'm referring to revenge.

Legally, there are governing rules by which to pursue legal rights in retaining payment for services rendered—which I ended up doing after I was able to work through my motives—but that is different from revenge. Revenge is defined as "inflicting punishment in return for injury or insult; seeking or taking vengeance for oneself or another." Justice, on the other hand, is defined as "the quality of being just; fairness, the principle of moral rightness; equity." Justice is supported by proof of an infraction with potential restitution by legal means. Revenge is a personal infraction with restitution by one's own means. The true difference between justice and revenge begins with the motives of the heart.

LOOKING AT THE HEART

Scripture refers to the condition of the heart hundreds of times. It is one of the most powerful aspects of who we are as human beings. Scripture tells us that we are blessed when our heart is pure (Matthew 5:8). Murder and adultery begin in the heart (Matthew 5:21-22, 27-28). Our treasure is in our hearts (Matthew 6:21). "Out of the abundance of the heart the mouth speaks" (Matthew 12:34). "Out of the heart come evil thoughts, murder, adultery, sexual immorality, theft, false witness, slander" (Matthew 15:19). Forgiveness comes from the heart (Matthew 18:35).

We reason in our hearts (Mark 2:8). Wisdom can enter our hearts, and we can apply it to our hearts to retain understanding (Proverbs 2:2, 10). Our hearts keep the commands of God (Proverbs 3:1), and we can write his commands on our hearts (Proverbs 3:3). These are just a handful of things the heart has the power to do.

Knowing our heart has the power to sway our behavior, we must consider it a priority to keep an eye on what we allow to come into our hearts. In his book *Christ-Centered Therapy*, Neil Anderson warns us:

> The human heart is . . . difficult to define. It seems to be the core of our inner being. Consider the proverb of Solomon: "As water reflects a face, so a man's heart reflects the man" (Proverbs 27:19). New Testament professor Robert Jewett gives further explanation: "A characteristic of the heart as the center of man is its inherent openness to outside impulses, its directionality, its propensity to give itself to a master and to live towards some desired goal." There is truth in this description, because we are not the source of our own life. Rather, we are dependent creatures who by nature look outside ourselves for life. What the heart takes in also becomes its master, stamping the heart with its character.[8]

Dr. Anderson's words ring loud and clear in the silence of the soul. What we put into our hearts is what we get out of them. Thus we must be cautious with and aware of what we perceive and receive from external sources. A battle ensues when we have both the Word of God written on our hearts from time spent with him in prayer and in his Word but have also accepted information from the world.

This duality often rears its ugly head when the heart has been pierced by external circumstances, responding internally with rage and a desire to obtain revenge. Scripture affirms to us that we must beware of having a double heart. Psalm 28:3 tells us that evil can reside in our hearts, and Psalm 55:21 tell us war can occur there. We see evidence of this duality daily, but to me it's most prevalent in divorce courts. It's amazing to me how two people can be so madly in love and repeat vows to love and cherish one another one year, only to seek to destroy each other a few years later. How can the heart be overflowing with love and be willing to die for the other person one year and be full of hate and retaliation the next? As a counselor for children for over a decade, I have stood in many courtrooms during divorce proceedings. I hope I never see this duality again.

I've heard story after story in court of one mate attempting to kill the other or gossiping about and slandering the other, parents accusing the other of sexually assaulting their child or sabotaging the other's relationship with a child, and so on, all in an attempt to harm the other person because the husband or wife or both felt hurt—not out of a concern for truth. I can't tell you how many times I've walked out of court with a weeping child who was forever damaged by the shrapnel from a full-out assault by one parent toward the other. It's horrific.

Contrary to popular belief, the dominant function of the heart is not an emotional one. According to the Bible, the heart has three primary functions. First, it's the place where we think; second, it's where we exercise the will; and, third, it's where we feel. Because it's the sphere where we think, we are commanded to take every thought captive to the obedience of Christ (2 Corinthians 10:5). In doing so, our own will (as we discussed in relation to God's will in Chapter Seven) must come into submission to God's will. In further concession, our emotions will respond to that which we think and will. In other words, our thoughts are the engine of the train that rolls down the track, our will is the freight car, and our emotions are the caboose. But what does all of this have to do with revenge and retaliation? Everything.

When we become hurt or offended by another, we tend to nurse negative thoughts toward the offender. We reenact the details of the offense in our mind over and over, reiterating our right to be offended and re-traumatizing ourselves in the process. We may also retell the story over and over to others in an attempt to get them to jump on the bandwagon of resentment toward the other person, and that tactic often works. As we do so, we water any existing seeds of anger, resentment, and bitterness, causing them to take root in our hearts. In that way, we justify retaliation. We feed our will within, and as a result we desire to harm the other person. Revenge stems from unresolved anger, hatred, bitterness, and unforgiveness. When nurtured in the mind, these emotions build; and once they reach the boiling point, retaliation is only an opportunity away.

I recently watched a woman on television whose daughter had been killed by her son-in-law. Rightfully so, the woman was in great despair. She wanted the young man who'd murdered her daughter to die for what he'd done. Legally that was an option in this case. Because of the brutality of the offense, he was charged with first-degree murder and was given the death penalty. None of this so far was vengeful. It was the fulfillment of the law. However, that same night I saw another interview with the mother. She was asked if she was finally at peace, knowing that the man who'd killed her daughter was going to die. Her answer was no. She knew that even if he died that very day, that wouldn't bring her daughter back to life. Then the woman went into a description of what she'd like to see done to the man—specifically, what *she'd* like to do to the man if given the chance. Her words and thoughts stemmed from revenge, hatred, unforgiveness, and bitterness. I understand as a mother why she feels so strongly about this, but I'd like to shed a little further light on the situation.

The perpetrator in this case never shed a tear in any of the footage regarding the case. As a matter of fact, he smiled almost the entire time the camera was on him, which I'm confident fed his mother-in-law's hatred. It seemed that he couldn't have cared less about what he'd done and the sentence given to him by the court. He'd gone on with his life (as much as he could in prison) despite what he'd done, and the death penalty sentence didn't seem to bother him in any way. Her hatred toward him, her words of revenge that poured out of her mouth, her unforgiveness didn't have any effect on him, but all the while they were eating her up inside. Let me explain.

Most individuals mistakenly believe that if we work toward letting go of the bitterness, hatred, and unforgiveness we have toward someone, we are saying that what the other person did was okay. What this young man did by killing this woman's daughter can never be justified, no matter how you look at it. It was wrong—100 percent wrong—and he needs to be held accountable for his actions (and he is). But by holding onto unforgiveness in her heart, the mother is ensnaring herself, not the son-in-law. Not only is *he* living with the consequences of his behavior, but so is she. She may believe she's further punishing him by refusing to forgive, remaining full of rage, hatred, bitterness, and unforgiveness. But these feelings will kill *her* if she doesn't process them. Doing so in no way justifies what that man did. But it will enable her to separate her grief over her daughter's death from her responsive emotions to the crime and its perpetrator and will give her an aspect of freedom so she is able to grieve and heal.

Additionally, working through the bitterness and unforgiveness is not an invitation for the person to hurt us again, nor does it give us reason to trust him again. Let me give you an example. As I mentioned in a previous chapter, I was sexually abused while growing up. As an adult I worked through those tough issues and eventually began working as a co-therapist with Dr. Jim Vigorito, who specializes in relapse prevention, working with male sex offenders. As I worked with these men, some of whom had received Christ as their Savior, I really struggled with the issue of whether I could or should trust them. I told Dr. Vigorito, "While I believe God has forgiven them, I sure wouldn't trust them to baby-sit my child." In a spirit of grace, which those who know Dr. Vigorito see an abundance of in his life, he gave me some of the wisest advice I've ever heard. He said, "Leslie, regardless of what these men have ever done, if they've asked Jesus into their hearts as their Savior, he has forgiven them, and they are saved. That, however, does not restore the trust they've broken. There are natural consequences to what we do on earth. For these men, one aspect of this is that they may never be allowed to be around children again." His answer rang true in my spirit.

God's forgiveness and ours does not automatically instill a full tank of trust in the heart of the community or in the relationship with the one wounded. When I was going through my divorce after my husband had been so horrifically abusive and had been so blatantly unfaithful, he told me he was sorry and asked my forgiveness. It took me a long time to work through my pain and forgive him, but when I did so, I called him and shared that step with him. As a result, he told me I had to trust him from that point forward to never harm me again physically or to cheat on me. He demanded that we remarry and said that in doing so I was giving him "the gift of trust," which would indeed prove my forgiveness. But that was an attempt to further manipulate me. Perhaps he would never harm me or be unfaithful again, but I could not be so foolish as to trust that blindly. And that's not unforgiveness—that's wisdom.

Forgiveness is not as hard as we sometimes make it. It simply means that we give up our right to hold on to the sinful actions of others against us internally. Forgiveness has less to do with the person who harmed us than it has to do with us. By giving up our right to hold on to others' wrongdoings against us, we do not necessarily release them of their responsibility. I forgave my ex-husband for breaking my back, but I still hold him responsible for the doctor bills accumulated by the break. The woman who forgave her son-in-law for murdering her daughter does not have to advocate for his release from prison. The man who forgives his father for molesting his daughter does not have to invite him to the child's birthday party every year. You can release persons from their debt against you but still hold them to the natural consequences. Consider salvation in relation to this topic.

I often visit inmates in prisons around America and share the saving knowledge of Jesus Christ with them. As a result I see thousands of men and women make a confession of faith every year. When they do so, they are forgiven of every sin they've ever committed, but we do not open the prison gates and set them free. They still have to live out the natural consequences of their sin. Equally so, when we receive Jesus as our Savior and are forgiven of all our sins, there are still residual consequences we have to endure. The sex addict, forgiven of his infidelities, may have to deal with the consequences of having a sexually transmitted disease for the remainder of his years. The gambling addict, although forgiven, may spend twenty years paying off his debtors. The woman who wrote thousands of dollars worth of bad checks, although saved, may have to make restitution for many years. The man who had a child out of wedlock but gets saved is forgiven for having premarital sex, but he is still responsible for that child's support and welfare.

This is not to say that grace does not prevail. The biggest manifestation of grace is found in forgiveness, and there may be times when God specifically tells us to advocate against consequences for someone, but we must be sure that is his will in those circumstances. It is easy to cover codependency with a blanket of grace, but that just enables unhealthy behavior to continue. Scripture tells us that our Father corrects his children because he loves them. Consequences are a part of correction, can prevent others from being harmed, and can humble a wicked heart to bring it to a place of transformation. Part of what enables us to work through tough issues toward someone who has harmed us is believing and trusting God to be our defender and the One who will repay the evil that has been done to us.

LET VENGEANCE BE GOD'S

We must surrender our own desires to God's, and we read in Romans 12 that it's God's will for us *not* to take revenge but to allow room for his wrath to present itself in our offender's life. "Beloved, never avenge yourselves, but leave it to the wrath of God, for it is written, 'Vengeance is mine, I will repay, says the Lord'" (v. 19). This proclamation of truth leads us back to the Garden of Gethsemane, where the physician Luke shares the reaction of Jesus' disciples when the army of soldiers came to the Garden to arrest him:

> *And when those who were around him saw what would follow, they said, "Lord, shall we strike with the sword?" And one of them struck the servant of the high priest and cut off his right ear. But Jesus said, "No more of this!" And he touched his ear and healed him. (Luke 22:49-51)*

Matthew tells us that the person who drew his sword was the impulsive Peter, and he depicts a very important statement by Jesus not included in Luke's description of the story:

> *"Put your sword back into its place. For all who take the sword will perish by the sword. Do you think that I cannot appeal to my Father, and he will at once send me more than twelve legions of angels?" (26:52-53)*

Jesus reproved Peter for striking the servant of the high priest, adding, "all who take the sword will perish by the sword." The sword has a legitimate role in the world. Scripture tells us that it can be used righteously, in defense of our lives, families, and nation and in various other necessary aspects on earth, but the sword is not to be used in vengeance. Our own unresolved issues with God cannot justify bloodshed and harm to others, and that's exactly what unforgiveness, bitterness, and hatred are—not conflict with another person but with God. When we bathe in revenge, hatred, bitterness, and unforgiveness, we are doing so in direct violation of God's Word, which tells the believer to walk in peace, love, patience, kindness, and more (1 Corinthians 13). It's a conflict between you and the offender only after you walk in disobedience to God.

I'm confident that I'm not winning any popularity contests with these words, but they are true. This is coming from a woman who wrestles day and night with these horrific issues. Scripture admonishes us to "pray without ceasing" (1 Thessalonians 5:17). I've learned to do that merely from grappling with this area of my life. No battles in my life have been as bloody or have had as many casualties as those that stemmed out of my revengeful heart. I have had to learn that the weapons of the Christian warfare are not physical but spiritual, and we must maintain that perspective (2 Corinthians 10:4).

As children of the King, we have the right, as Jesus did, to call on our Father, and he will put at our disposal his armies of angels. But he will do so only if that is *his* will, not ours. Jesus knew that it was God's will for him to be arrested, knowing it would lead to his sacrifice for us; thus he didn't request an angelic rescue. We know that God's will is for us to allow him to handle vengeance against our foes. We must understand that our enemies are his enemies and vice versa, and in turn surrendering to his will is to take him at his word.

11

The Fulfillment of a Promise

I consider that the sufferings of this present time are not worth comparing with the glory that is to be revealed to us.

ROMANS 8:18

On a night over two thousand years ago our Lord and Savior, Jesus Christ, journeyed into a garden with several companions. This was no ordinary garden. There was an olive press, surrounded by gnarled olive trees, but it would not be the tender fruit that would be crushed that night, but the spirit of the Son of God. He would not just suffer but would agonize over the mission at hand, the horrific events yet to come, and the torture that his spirit, mind, emotions, and body would endure.

The overwhelming load of all of humanity's sins were upon him. It would be one of hell's most triumphant hours, appearing to be a victory to all those who witnessed it in both the human and spirit realms. Humanity would join in the hellish celebration, destroying the flesh of our Savior, mocking his royalty, and scorning his power. When Jesus died, by all external evidence the bad guy had won the battle. But that was not the end of the story.

Jesus endured, persevered, and overcame the agony of the Garden and of his death (which lasted for only a short time) for the glory of the cross, which we know is eternal. When we received Christ as our Savior, we made a vow, a covenant, to become one with him and his sufferings. In essence, when we accepted Jesus as our Savior we said the very thing the apostle Paul said in Philippians 3:10: "I want to know Christ and the power of his resurrection and the fellowship of sharing in his sufferings, becoming like him in his death" (NIV).

Nowhere does the Bible teach that Christians are to be exempt from suffering. As a matter of fact, Jesus told his disciples that the world would hate them, that they would be "as sheep in the midst of wolves" (Matthew 10:16). They would be arrested, scourged, brought before governors and kings, and accused falsely. Even their loved ones would persecute them. The apostle Paul had a lot to say about believers' suffering. He made it crystal-clear that being a child of God means that we will endure difficulty on earth. In Romans 8:17 he tells us, "Now if we are children, then we are heirs—heirs of God and co-heirs with Christ, if indeed we share in his sufferings in order that we may also share in his glory."

Paul was not a sadomasochist. He knew the secret to suffering that I commented on in the introduction of this book. He was familiar with the knowledge that suffering on earth is only for a season and that believers will join in Jesus' glory, promise, and resurrection for eternity. He also knew what Jesus proclaimed time and time again through his life on earth—that when we die to ourselves and our own will, we enjoy eternal life; that in the midst of turmoil and heart-wrenching chaos, we can attain God's peace; that when we are faced with physical death, we receive eternal life; and that in the midst of grappling with sorrow, we find intimacy with God. These seemingly contradictory statements are complex to the finite mind and offensive to those who are perishing spiritually but are soothing to believers. We have comfort, rest, and hope in Christ regardless of our circumstances.

Many of our forefathers knew this secret to suffering. Early Christians rejoiced in suffering because they looked at it in the light of eternity. It is said that when Ignatius was about to die for his faith in A.D. 110 he cried out, "Near to the sword, near to God; in company with wild beasts, in company with God." Similarly, the apostle Paul, writing from a prison in Rome, boldly wrote, "I want you to know, brothers, that what has happened to me [imprisonment] has really served to advance the gospel" (Philippians 1:12).

When I think about suffering and various stories in the Bible, I often consider Job, who was delivered into the hands of Satan to prove he was not serving God simply because God had blessed him (Job 1:8-12; 2:3-6). In his suffering Job asked the rhetorical question, "If a man dies, shall he live again? All the days of my service I would wait, till my renewal should come" (14:14). Job knew his suffering was temporary and would cease at some point in the future. Waiting for Christ's return gave him hope.

> For I know that my Redeemer lives,
> and at the last he will stand upon the earth.
> And after my skin has been thus destroyed,
> yet in my flesh I shall see God,
> whom I shall see for myself,
> and my eyes shall behold, and not another.
> My heart faints within me! (19:25-27)

Job knew that the Redeemer who had purchased him from the slavery of sin had not forgotten him even though he was suffering tremendously. Jesus encourages us not to let our hearts be troubled but to trust in our Father (John 14:1). He promises us that our trials will someday end, at which point we will be with God forever. Let's briefly look at how Job specifically chose to handle his suffering and at the result of his commitment to stand on God's promises.

Satan accused Job before God (1:9-11), took his worldly wealth (1:13-17), and killed all his children (1:18-19). He struck Job with boils and sores (2:7) and caused the shedding of bleached skin, fever, and chills (30:30), intolerable itching, swollen limbs, ulcers that bred maggots (7:5), halitosis (19:17), choking, corroding bones, diarrhea, feelings of panic (21:6), depression, and terrifying nightmares that led to insomnia. Job's wife ridiculed him and encouraged him to curse God (2:9), and his friends accused him of sin that he had not committed (4:8). In response to all of this, Scripture tells us that Job prayed (10:2), praised God (10:8), and prayed some more (13:20). He hoped in the Lord (13:15), trusted in his Redeemer (19:25), and proclaimed God's righteousness (Job 23).

Nehemiah was another man who endured great suffering. His enemies ridiculed him (Nehemiah 2:19), mocked him (4:1-3), conspired to attack him and to create confusion (4:7-8), oppressed him (5:1-5), plot-ted to harm him (6:1-2), and developed a plot to discredit him (6:10-14). Nehemiah, in response, prayed (1:11), and prayed (4:4-5), and prayed (4:9), and prayed (6:9), and prayed (6:14). Nehemiah took other action as well, and there were other attempts from his enemies to bring him harm, but Nehemiah did not take action without first consulting God through prayer.

In response to both of these men, God was faithful and blessed them immensely. I wouldn't have blamed either man if he had handled things differently, but both kept their focus on the eternal prize rather than on their current circumstances.

The Bible teaches that every believer who is faithful to Christ must be prepared to suffer. Second Timothy 3:12 tells us, "Indeed, all who desire to live a godly life in Christ Jesus will be persecuted." Instead of looking at suffering only as an affliction, Jesus told his followers to see it from a godly perspective, as a blessing. They were to "rejoice and be glad" when persecuted (Matthew 5:12). In doing so, they would understand another part of the secret—sometimes struggle and difficulty, pain and sorrow can be gifts.

THE GIFT OF SORROW

"You're kidding me, right?" a woman asked from the front row of the Bible study I was teaching in my home. "Sorrow can be a gift? It's not a gift I ever want to receive!" The other women in the class nodded their heads in agreement. I understood how they felt. It seems a ludicrous thing to say, but it's true. God uses heartache, sorrow, difficulties, and pain both to draw us closer to him and to give us hope. Dallas Anderson, who shared his "now and not yet" perspective with us earlier, puts it this way:

> God uses pain and suffering to create in each of us a longing for something more than this world has to offer. In that way it can actually be seen as a gift of sorts. If we never experienced pain and suffering we would never yearn for more than what we retain here on earth. God, in his ultimate wisdom, uses heartache and sorrow to create and nurture a longing for eternal things.

Dallas's words are true. I often long for a day that Scripture promises us will come—a day when death has no sting, age has no effect, sickness and disease are obsolete, and sin and its effects are absent. His words bear more truth than the obvious. Suffering is a gift because it purifies us and is the conduit for perfection. Christ maintained perfection in Gethsemane despite his suffering. In the most horrific of all circumstances, when the breath of death hovered over him, insurmountable agony inflicted him, the weight of the world's sin pressed upon him, and all of the power of hell violently assaulted him, he remained committed to his Father first and foremost and then to us.

All of creation and the powers of heaven stood ready for him to give the word, any word that would set them in motion to bring it all to an end in an instant. But he endured faithfully, keeping his eye on the prize. You see, Jesus knew there was more to the story than the agony he was enduring and the crushing of his spirit, soul, and body yet to come. Jesus knew the secret to suffering, which is a blatant absurdity to the human condition. Namely, in death we find life; in turmoil we find peace; one must lose one's life to gain it; and in the midst of severe heartache and struggle we find that which is irrepressible in the human spirit and always there in our relationship with God, the truth that although all of life is falling down around us and we feel like any second the foundation on which we stand will crumble beneath the weight of our crisis, we stand on the Cornerstone that the world rejected, a Rock that cannot crumble. Yes, there was Good Friday, a day where the end looked imminent, but there was also Easter Sunday, where we learn that Good Friday was not the end but the beginning.

When I was pregnant with my daughter, Charlene, I couldn't wait to give birth for the first time and experience this new life. A month past my due date, the doctors induced labor. I was excited and eager to see the child I'd been carrying for over nine months. They administered a drug called Pitocin. Once it entered my body and I experienced my first contraction, I wasn't so excited about induced labor. Hours later, with contractions a minute apart, I was willing to be pregnant for the rest of my life if only the pain would subside. It seemed like forever before the doctors allowed me to push and my beautiful daughter was born.

Naturally, the pain I'd experienced was eventually overshadowed by the beauty of my child and the experience of being a first-time mom. That was twenty-three years ago, and I don't remember the suffering. I know I went through excruciating pain, but I have no memory of the anguish my body went through. Someday, on the other side of eternity, we will have a similar experience. We will know what we endured, but we will not remember the anguish because we will be basking in the glory of God. We can taste some of that glory even now as we rest in the arms of our loving heavenly Father.

Brothers and sisters, I share your agony over your current circumstances although I do not know what they are. I do know that living today may be hard, and I cannot promise you that tomorrow will be easier. But I can say that when you are weak, your Savior is strong. Tear down the doors of heaven with your cries, flood the threshing floor with your tears, and resist any anger toward the One who can best comfort you in this time. Crawl onto his lap and nestle close enough to hear his heart, for it is from there that he speaks. Listen to him tell you that today is only one day in a lifetime, a small fragment of eternity. Hear him tell you that he has plans for you, for good and not for evil, to give you a hope and a future. He is telling you that there's more to your story than just yesterday and today.

Go to him boldly every day, and ask him to show you what that story entails. His mercies are new every morning. He will give you enough manna to strengthen you for today's battle. He will give you tools to use to fight against the lies of the enemy who whispers that there is no hope, no restoration, and no reason to go on. The devil is a liar, and the truth is not in him. I know. I've been caught in his web of deceit too many times. Clarity is found in God's truth, in God's promises, in his Word. Write his Word on your heart, and it will not be long before it becomes real to you.

Conclusion

I still hate suffering. I don't think it'll ever be something I'll enjoy going through. Suffering has taught me some pretty crucial lessons though. For one thing, I've learned to really appreciate those days, months, and years in life when it seems like I'm living on the mountaintop and beyond all the pain and anguish that humanity seems to bring on itself. And although past experience and current reality whisper the truth to me— that the valleys will come, that they will be dark and will try to consume me—I know also that I can endure them through Christ who strengthens me daily.

Second, I've learned that even in the midst of the most horrific circumstances, God's grace is present. He only allows us to endure that which he empowers us to overcome. We see evidence of God's grace in Job 1:10, where Satan refers to a "hedge" that God had put around Job and his family and his belongings. We too have a hedge around us that cannot be penetrated without God's permission. He is holding back an onslaught from the pit of hell that really would overcome and consume us. This grace becomes evident when we learn of the lives of others and how they have overcome seemingly insurmountable circumstances and odds.

The biographies that become best sellers, the movies that become blockbusters, and the heroes we admire the most are the ones we relate to—ordinary people who have overcome extraordinary odds, the underdog who becomes a champion, the wheelchair-bound Olympian, the man who came from an obscure background and rose to the top, the ugly duckling who becomes a beauty queen, the woman who endures abuse and becomes an advocate for others. While those examples deserve kudos, there is one story that far exceeds all others—the innocent man who was beaten to a pulp and hung on a cross and died, who rose from the dead three days later to save all of humanity from their sins. It's his story and the triumph over his suffering that gives us strength to do the same.

I've also learned that it is in the valleys, when my circumstances have stripped me of all my pretensions and pride, in the state of humility that surrounds me, I find the real me, a woman who lives and breathes for one purpose and one purpose only—to honor and glorify her King. Apart from that state of humility found in sorrow, I begin to believe the lie that I can do life in my own strength, on my own terms, and I set myself up for failure. It is during those moments of meekness that I hear his voice the clearest, feel his love the deepest, and understand his purpose. Those are the times that I want never to leave his presence. I beg him not to make me dwell in the humanity of life, knowing I will fail him, knowing I'll grow weak and frail in my attempts to overcome life. I want to rest in his presence and avoid the spiritual war at hand and its by-product, sin.

Finally, I've learned that suffering is just for a season. In the midst of the winter we long for spring, never really believing it will come. We think, *What if spring really doesn't come?* even though it has arrived winter after winter for all the years preceding this one. All we know is what we are experiencing right now, but spring will come in one way or another—if not in this lifetime, then in the one on the other side of eternity.

I anticipate that the Lord will teach me more lessons from suffering in the years to come. I'm forty years old, and apart from the Lord's taking me home to heaven, it is likely I will taste more heartache on a grand scale. Because I expect it, I can anticipate it and prepare for it by strengthening myself in God's Word, recalling all the ways he's been faithful to me and dwelling in his presence.

I do not know your story or the heartaches you've endured, but our Father knows it all intricately. Knowing that, I'll petition him daily on your behalf. As I wrote this book and long after the ink has dried, I will pray that you will find comfort in the arms of your Redeemer, healing in his presence, strength in his Word, and intimacy with him and with others through your struggle.

NOTES

1. "Regional Variations in Suicide Rates—United States, 1990-1994," Centers for Disease Control and Prevention, *MMWR* (*Morbidity and Mortality Weekly Report*), August 29, 1997, 46 (34): 789-792.
2. Ibid.
3. Injury Statistics Query and Reporting System (2002), National Center for Injury Prevention and Control, Centers for Disease Control and Prevention, March 27, 2003.
4. Ibid.
5. C. S. Lewis, *A Grief Observed* (New York: HarperCollins, 2001), p. 6.
6. Ken Gire, *Incredible Moments with the Savior* (Grand Rapids, MI: Zondervan, 1990), pp. 96-97, adapted.
7. *Key Word Study Bible* (Chattanooga: AMG Publishers, 1998).
8. See Neil T. Anderson, Terry E. Zuehlke, and Julianne S. Zuehlke, *Christ-Centered Therapy* (Grand Rapids, MI: Zondervan, 2000).

Fear not, for I have redeemed you;
I have called you by name, you are mine.
When you pass through the waters, I will be with you;
and through the rivers, they shall not overwhelm you;
when you walk through fire you shall not be burned,
and the flame shall not consume you.
For I am the LORD your God,
the Holy One of Israel, your Savior.

ISAIAH 43:1-3

If you would like to contact the author, you can reach her in the following ways:

By letter:

> Leslie Montgomery
> The Pool at Bethesda Ministries
> 19491 449th Avenue
> Lake Norden, South Dakota 57248

By e-mail:

> princesswarrior@lesliemontgomery.com
> Via the Internet:
> www.lesliemontgomery.com

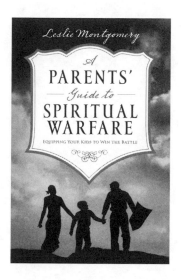

A Parents' Guide to Spiritual Warfare

Leslie Montgomery

This book vividly portrays the passion, heartache, and struggle that every parent deals with when raising a child, and the relentless attack against the family unit, specifically against children.

TPB, ISBN 1-58134-771-5